CW01465658

Progress You Can See

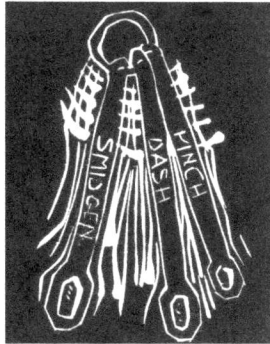

Artwork by: Shanna Ratner

I would like to dedicate this book to all courageous, wise, and hopeful social change agents around the world willing to think in systems, see the scope of what needs to be done, find the leverage points, and work collaboratively across boundaries for real and measurable change, and to all the Measurement Guides I have had the privilege of working with in person. I hope the lessons I have learned will resonate with you and shed light upon your path. Thank you.

Praise for this book

'Too often, decisions with societal impact are made without enough information and unintended consequences result. Ratner provides the clear path forward with how measuring for social change is not only possible but provides powerful clarity for moving forward. Bravo, and long needed!'

Rhonda Phillips, Ph.D., FAICP, President, Chatham University

'This is a very important book. "What we measure is what we do" is an important guide for social change. Shanna Ratner presents an approach to measuring that can involve entire communities in setting up and implementing measurement plans to determine if actions are meeting the goals of community improvement. The book is readable with examples that can serve as inspiration and ways of developing measurement plans that are doable on a local level and can be shared and discussed community-wide. As a community development practitioner, Shanna Ratner shares her experiences applying You Get What You Measure in a variety of contexts. Indicators of progress must be developed in context to be locally meaningful and motivating, which involves local data gathering as a critical part of the social change process.'

Cornelia Butler Flora, Distinguished Professor of Sociology Emerita,
Iowa State University and Research Professor,
Kansas State University

'In general, implementing a Strengths Based Approach requires belief in the approach, the courage to challenge traditional ways of thinking and working, as well as consistency in applying the approach over time. This book has inspired me to continue building a better positive future everywhere.'

Dani Wahyu Munggoro, Inspirasi Tanpa Batas (INSPIRIT), Indonesia

'The greatest shift in any age, the greatest disruption, comes in changing the way we think, opening ourselves up to different ways of seeing, of understanding. Shanna Ratner's Progress You Can See is a guide for that essential change in mindset. Practical, clear, inspired, read this book, and reimagine the power of what's possible in your community in the 21st century.'

Peter Smith, Executive & Creative Director,
Canadian Centre for Rural Creativity

'Shanna's work here is much more than a resource full of evaluation tools-it's a multi-dimensional and deeply impactful framework for learning how to measure whatever it is that matters to your work. This guide has helped me learn new ways of describing what I've always felt to be important in my work but struggled to put into words, it has shown me new tools to better capture the overall impact of Kitchen Sync Strategies' work, and it has helped me envision a future where our Measurement and evaluation processes can capture the complexities of truly transformative systems change work.'

Elliott Smith, CEO, Kitchen Sync Strategies

'As we strive to develop a more inclusive society and decision-making processes, Ratner's book provides a practical approach to measuring our learning and progress.'

Al Lauzon, Professor - Capacity Development & Extension,
University of Guelph

'Shanna Ratner has written a fascinating and important book—a must read for those who are committed to social change. Filled with practical examples and experiences, the book provides a compelling case for the importance of measuring progress towards social change goals and the need for a values-based, participatory, and systems-oriented approach to measurement that enables continuous learning and improvement.'

Yogesh Ghore, St. Francis Xavier University

Progress You Can See

Measuring for social change

Shanna E. Ratner

**Practical
ACTION
PUBLISHING**

Practical Action Publishing Ltd
25 Albert Street, Rugby,
Warwickshire, CV21 2SD, UK
www.practicalactionpublishing.com

© Shanna E. Ratner, 2023

The moral right of the author to be identified as author of the work
have been asserted under sections 77 and 78 of the Copyright Design and
Patents Act 1988.

All rights reserved. No part of this publication may be reprinted or
reproduced or utilized in any form or by any electronic, mechanical, or
other means, now known or hereafter invented, including photocopying
and recording, or in any information storage or retrieval system, without the
written permission of the publishers. Product or corporate names may be
trademarks or registered trademarks, and are used only for identification and
explanation without intent to infringe.

Product or corporate names may be trademarks or registered trademarks, and
are used only for identification and explanation without intent to infringe.

A catalogue record for this book is available from the British Library.

A catalogue record for this book has been requested from the Library of
Congress.

ISBN 978-1-78853-252-5 Paperback
ISBN 978-1-78853-253-2 Hardback
ISBN 978-1-78853-254-9 Electronic book

Citation: Ratner, S.E., (2023) *Progress You Can See: Measuring for social change*,
Rugby, UK: Practical Action Publishing <http://doi.org/10.3362/9781788532549>.

Since 1974, Practical Action Publishing has published and disseminated
books and information in support of international development work
throughout the world. Practical Action Publishing is a trading name of
Practical Action Publishing Ltd (Company Reg. No. 1159018), the wholly
owned publishing company of Practical Action. Practical Action Publishing
trades only in support of its parent charity objectives and any profits are
covenanted back to Practical Action (Charity Reg. No. 247257, Group VAT
Registration No. 880 9924 76).

The views and opinions in this publication are those of the author and do
not represent those of Practical Action Publishing Ltd or its parent charity
Practical Action.

Reasonable efforts have been made to publish reliable data and information,
but the authors and publisher cannot assume responsibility for the validity
of all materials or for the consequences of their use.

Cover artwork by Shanna E. Ratner. Cover Design by Katarzyna Markowska,
Practical Action Publishing
Typeset by vPrompt eServices, India

Contents

List of figures, exercises, and boxes   xi

Acknowledgements   xiii

Preface   xv

Chapter 1   Introduction   1
    Origins of you get what you measure   1
    Conclusion   10
    How to use this book   11

Chapter 2   Why measure?   17
    Precision in measurement   18
    How the process of measurement helps us learn   20
    Testing assumptions   20
    Fuelling continuous learning through reflection   21
    Information flow   22
    Capturing the results of experimentation and mitigating risk   27
    A note on accountability   27
    Supporting self-organizing behaviour   29
    Helping us tell our stories   30

Chapter 3   Measurement vocabulary and an overview of
                    the measurement process   33
    Goal   33
    Indicator   35
    Assumption   36
    Measure   37
    Action   37
    An overview of the measurement process   37
    Communication skills   40

Chapter 4   Getting to goals   43
    Values   43
    Themes   43
    Goals   44

Chapter 5   Indicators of progress   51
    The power of visualization in social change work   51
    The definition and form of an indicator   52

Chapter 6   Indicator analysis for ordinary people   59
    Analysing indicators in a systems context   62

Chapter 7   Creating measures that matter   77
    What is a measure?   77
    How do we create measures that matter?   78
    Begin at the end   88
    Influencing decision-makers   91

Chapter 8   Developing a measurement plan   95
    Units of measure   95
    Establishing a baseline   97
    Framing measures: understanding what's possible   99
    The measurement plan   102

Chapter 9   Getting the information you need   111
    Measurement methods   111
    Testing the measurement plan   120

Chapter 10   Actions – re-measurement – interpretation   123
    Acting for impact   123
    Re-measurements   130
    Interpreting the results of measurement   132
    Conclusion   134

Appendix 1   Causal looping   137
Appendix 2   Suggestions for implementing the YGWYM
    approach virtually   141
Appendix 3   Links to video content linked to book chapters   149

List of figures, exercises and boxes

List of figures

Figure 1.1	Sample workshop evaluation form	14
Figure 1.2	Creating our own ground rules worksheet	15
Figure 2.1	Everyday measurement worksheet	19
Figure 3.1	Measurement vocabulary handout	38
Figure 3.2	Overview of the measurement process	39
Figure 4.1	Sample values to themes to goals, South Wood, 2009	48
Figure 6.1	Everyday assumptions worksheet	61
Figure 6.2	Indicator analysis	64
Figure 6.3	Mapping the impact of key leverage indicators (KLI) on the whole system	67
Figure 6.4	Byways indicator analysis	69
Figure 6.5	Indicator analysis in PowerPoint	73
Figure 6.6	Indicator analysis in Excel	74
Figure 9.1	Roles in the research continuum	113
Figure A1	Supply/demand relationship for corn	138
Figure A2	Virus transmission loop	139
Figure A3	Exercise loop	139

List of exercises

Exercise 3.1	Skilled listening and skilled inquiry	42
Exercise 4.1	Values to themes	45
Exercise 4.2	Themes to goals	47
Exercise 5.1	Guided visualization	52
Exercise 5.2	Developing and clarifying indicators	56
Exercise 6.1	Everyday assumptions	60
Exercise 6.2	Analysing indicators in a systems context	62
Exercise 6.3	Capturing assumptions	65
Exercise 6.4	'Scoring' the indicator analysis	66
Exercise 10.1	Aligning YGWYM actions with current activities	129

List of boxes

Box 7.1   The power of measures in aligning actions with goals:
                an example from the field   82

Box 8.1   Using measurement to help reduce residential water
                use in Colorado   104

Box 10.1   Framing a direct action to achieve a goal
                in the Virgin Islands   126

Acknowledgements

Many thanks to the first readers of this manuscript, Jeff Farbman, Sarah Rocker, and Nancy Orr, for their perceptive comments and suggested improvements. Thanks as well to Barbara Wyckoff, Steve Marshall, Yvonne D. Petersen, Jack Salo, Evan Smith, Mike McCarthy, and Kim Norris who graciously shared their You Get What You Measure (YGWYM) and related stories with me. Thank you to the Measurement Guides who agreed to have their Becoming a Measurement Guide training videotaped for posterity. The enthusiastic response to YGWYM from clients and Measurement Guides with whom I and my colleagues at Yellow Wood Associates, Inc. had the privilege of sharing this process over several decades are the reason this book exists. Your enthusiasm for YGWYM inspired me to make the process more widely available. Although there are too many of you to name individually, you know who you are. Thank you and may all your social change work be for a blessing. Thanks as well to Yellow Wood Associate Rob Petrini who came up with the Excel method for recording the results of the indicator analysis. Thanks as well to my son, Sam Ratner, whose support and encouragement mean the world.

Preface

The amount we know and understand about our world is dwarfed by the amount we do *not* know. We tend to assume that we know more, often a lot more, than we do. And what we think we know governs our behaviour. We make assumptions about ourselves as individuals. I 'know' that I cannot sing so I won't try. I 'know' that nothing will grow in my backyard, so I do not bother to figure out why not. We make assumptions about our relationships. If you do not answer my email, it must be because you do not want to communicate with me. If you live in that part of town, you must be well-educated. If you vote differently than I do, you must be an idiot or, at the very least, not well-informed.

We also make assumptions about what we know collectively. Even if I do not know the answer myself, someone knows, right? Surely by now we collectively know how the brain works, how the universe was formed, the most effective way to manage an economy, and how to best help someone with a learning disability. Not really. If you dig deeply enough into any subject and take the time to find the people who are most knowledgeable about it, they will tell you how much they do not know as well as what little they do.

We have a lot to learn as individuals and as a society. Measurement is first and foremost a tool for learning. It allows us to test our assumptions instead of allowing our assumptions to limit our sense of what is possible. Used properly, the process of measurement helps us create and express individual and collective curiosity about our circumstances and how we might improve them. It takes advantage of our diverse experiences to help us understand and alter the larger systems that determine our fate. *The purpose of measurement is to assist us in learning, focusing, and seeing systems so that we can improve our individual and collective ability to reach shared goals*. That is the focus of this book.

Who should read this book

This book is intended for anyone who is interested in a practical approach to seeing and analysing systems. It can be applied by just about anyone in any setting in which you can bring diverse stakeholders together. The measurement process described herein, called You Get What You Measure (YGWYM), was created and trademarked by the author, and tested in the field for over 25 years.[1] It does not require advanced degrees or mathematical prowess. Anyone can measure; in fact, all of us do it every day. YGWYM does require facilitation by a person or people who train themselves in the process laid out here. We call these people *Measurement Guides*. This book, and the accompanying videos, are intended as a self-guided training programme for Measurement Guides. Measurement Guides must have the requisite facilitation skills to work through this process with others. This book does not teach facilitation skills per se; rather the focus is on learning a process that requires them.

Progress You Can See provides readers with a step-by-step introduction to You Get What You Measure, a process for helping diverse groups identify goals, discover leverage indicators, development measures and focus their actions for social change. For many years, the author trained skilled facilitators to become Measurement Guides in face-to-face workshops called Becoming a Measurement Guide. People who purchase Progress You Can See have access to videotapes of a Becoming a Measurement Guide workshop led by the author in 2012. The tapes are organized to correspond with the chapters in Progress You Can See. The workshop is based on a case study and involves role playing. Viewers will be able to watch the author describing the process and learn from the experiences of the five workshop participants.

This book is particularly addressed to practitioners, funders, and other people who are committed, professionally and/or personally, to social change. I define social change as any effort to change the systems that govern our own and others' behaviours in such a way as to make the world a fairer, more equitable, kinder, safer, healthier, and more resilient place for all the people who live in it. In Hebrew it is called *Tikkun Olam* – to heal the world. In my experience there are many people trying to figure out how to leave the world a better place than they found it. This book is for you. This book offers a method for incorporating measurement intentionally into social change work without breaking the bank or being limited to data provided by others that may or may not be relevant to the work we are doing.

Social change practitioners work at many different scales, from local to international, and in many different fields from health care to transportation to manufacturing and so on. *The beauty of the process described in this book is that it is content and scale neutral.* You can bring your content to the process and it will work. One practitioner, who has used this process in a variety of settings from non-profits to government, asked me if I had ever known it to fail. I said 'no', and she concurred. There are benefits to be gained at every step, even if you never complete the entire process. You can even use it in your personal life. A colleague recently shared with me his decision to use this process to help himself gain clarity around his intentions and expectations related to transitioning from a full-time job outside the home to full-time parenting.

A different approach to measurement

Measurement, including, but not limited to statistics, can be used to intentionally mislead. Darrell Huff, in his famous book *How to Lie with Statistics*, shows many ways in which numbers can be used to convey misinformation. Often, however, we simply mislead ourselves by using or repeating numbers which we do not understand. To understand any statistic, we must know the basis on which it was derived, and for what purpose. Often, we have no idea. This means we also do not understand the extent to which numbers derived elsewhere can be meaningfully applied to our particular challenge or circumstance.

Nor do we understand the limits of that applicability. For example, in my work as an applied economist, I have often witnessed the misuse of economic multipliers. Economic multipliers are statistics derived from what are essentially 'black box' econometric models. Some of these models purport to measure the 'multiplier effect' of additional spending on income or jobs within a given geographic area. The larger the area in terms of square miles and population, everything else being equal, the more broadly accurate the multiplier is likely to be. This is because areas with significant population density and/or large regions (e.g. an entire state or multi-state area) provide many opportunities for spending and employment. Small areas, like, for example, a rural community or a rural county, provide relatively few options for spending and/or employment. Therefore, when a multiplier that has been derived for a large area is applied to a small area, it is misleading because it exaggerates the local impacts likely to occur from an incremental increase in earnings or jobs. If the opportunities for spending and employment are limited in the local area, it is highly likely that any jobs created and earnings spent will be outside the local area if at all. Developers seeking to generate support for their rural projects often use unrealistic multipliers to try to convince rural people of the benefits that will accrue to them as a result of the development in question. This is just another instance of lying with statistics.

This book is not about numbers or statistics, per se. Numbers and measurement are not the same thing. Measures may include numbers, but measurement for social change, when arrived at through the process described in this book, results in more than a statistic; it provides an intentional process to help us better understand the world around us by exploring specific assumptions in context. Measures that matter are those that have meaning for the people who construct, collect, and interpret them. There are many ways to measure: some involve instrumentation, others merely consistent observation. Measures that matter can be used over time to better understand the anticipated and unanticipated outcomes connected with the actions we take and the decisions we make in pursuit of social change. Without measures we have no way of knowing whether we are making a positive difference.

Developing measures in a systems context does not require a PhD in statistics. It does require willingness to define desired outcomes in measurable terms and then place those outcomes in context. It requires being willing to go beyond the information that may be readily available to gather the information we need to measure progress toward our goals. Most systems of measurement rely far too heavily on 'available data' and not nearly heavily enough on identifying and developing data that is truly relevant to the situation at hand. Pretty pictures of pie charts, bar graphs and other illustrations too often simplify data for presentation without examining the assumptions made in data interpretation. If we do not understand how the information that we rely on was collected, by whom, from whom, and for what purposes, we are apt to misapply it to our own situations and arrive at false interpretations of meaning.

Measurement as a process

YGWYM does not include a compendium of measures to choose from; rather it provides a process you can use to derive measures that are relevant for your own work. It is neither a silver bullet nor a shortcut to satisfying measurement requirements. Instead, it provides a process for designing measures that are directly connected to key leverage indicators that have been identified through participatory systems analysis as strongly related to specific goals. YGWYM has been in development and use for over 25 years with non-profits, federal, state, and local governments, citizens, groups, and professional organizations around the country and was featured in *The Nonprofit Outcomes Toolbox* by Robert M. Penna.[2]

The entire YGWYM process is about creating knowledge as well as accountability, but not accountability to funders per se. Accountability is established not by imposing numerical targets, but by building relationships and the capacity to collectively interpret new information among diverse stakeholders who share an interest in the same goal. Measures developed through the YGWYM process record behavioural changes (or the lack thereof) that relate to progress toward shared goals.

YGWYM benefits practitioners as well as funder/investors and increases our shared understanding of what works in relation to social change goals. By demystifying (but not oversimplifying) measurement, it unlocks the creativity and power inherent in thinking through not only what to measure but how to measure so that the very process of measuring contributes to progress toward the goal. It is *not* business as usual. If this process were widely adopted, I believe it would improve government, private, and not-for-profit organizations by reducing the waste associated with flawed approaches to measurement. It would also elevate awareness of whole systems and strategic pathways to systems change through effective partnerships.

Without measurement, we have no idea whether the actions we have chosen to take are making the difference that we intended. We do not know if things are changing for better or for worse. We are flying blind and all we have is hope or despair. Hope by itself will not help us get better at what we do, and despair is what happens when you are afraid that nothing you do matters. YGWYM helps us learn which activities are effective in moving us toward desired outcomes and which are not, it encourages mid-course corrections, and it improves the chances that we will be able to choose effective activities that allow us to make tangible progress toward desired outcomes over time. Measurement as described here can address both hope and despair, tempering collective despair and giving shape to shared hope.

Notes

1. The author has allowed Yellow Wood Associates' trademark for You Get What You Measure to lapse in anticipation of the publication of this book. Credit given to Yellow Wood Associates for use of the process as a whole or in part is always appreciated.
2. Penna, R.M. (2011) *The Nonprofit Outcomes Toolbox: A Complete Guide to Program Effectiveness, Performance Measurement, and Results*, John Wiley & Sons, Hoboken, NJ.

CHAPTER 1
Introduction

Origins of you get what you measure

I was one of about a dozen seasoned professionals who were invited to participate in the Aspen Institute's Learning Cluster on Community Capacity Building in the mid-1990s. The objective of the Learning Cluster was to elevate the importance of capacity building in community and economic development and show funders how capacity, which was always considered a soft and fuzzy concept, could be quantified and measured.

We defined community capacity as the combined influence of a community's commitment, resources, and skills that can be deployed to build on community strengths and address community problems and opportunities (Aspen Institute Rural Economic Policy Program, 1996). Then we went on to define eight outcomes of capacity. These were:

- expanding, diverse, inclusive citizen participation;
- expanding leadership base;
- strengthened individual skills;
- widely shared public understanding and vision;
- strategic community agenda;
- consistent, tangible progress toward goals;
- more effective community organizations and institutions;
- better use of resources by the community.

For each of these outcomes we developed indicators, sub-indicators, and sub-sub-indicators, and an array of measures that a practitioner could choose from to establish the status of a given indicator, sub-indicator or sub-sub-indicator. Essentially, this was a laundry list of measures.

This was okay as far as it went. It provided a conceptual framework and at least gave us a way to illustrate the potential for measuring community capacity. What it did not provide, however, was a *process* through which practitioners could define specific outcomes relevant to their own work, understand the factors influencing those outcomes, and find the leverage points in the systems influencing their work that had the greatest potential to drive the entire system toward their desired outcomes. It did not encourage practitioners to conceive of the measures most appropriate to their work or which measurement systems needed to be embedded in their work and the lives of their intended beneficiaries. Nor did it enable them to identify what was working well and what was not and determine whether progress was being made toward their goals. Finally, it did not shift the power to define relevant measures from the top to the bottom.

Powerful measurement begins with a process for thinking through the information you really need to make better decisions to enable you to make tangible progress toward the goals to which you are committed. Wasteful measurement results from being told what you need to measure for the purpose of being accountable to some person or entity who is essentially external to the system you need to change to make progress, and who may or may not be aware of the culture, vision, and mission that drives your work.

Based on over 35 years of experience in the field of rural economic development, I have concluded that, by and large, the way we approach measurement for social change leans toward wasteful and away from powerful. All too often, we fail to measure our impacts at all.

Many years ago, I worked on a project to understand the institutional arrangements that governed Lake Champlain, the sixth largest freshwater lake in the United States. Lake Champlain is bordered by New York, Vermont, and Quebec, Canada. One aspect of our study involved identifying all the international, federal, state and local governmental and non-profit organizations and institutions whose mission, whether scientific, recreational, governmental or other, had some connection to the lake, and asking them how their actions had impacted the lake over time. I was naïve enough to be shocked when I discovered that not a single governmental unit or non-profit had any idea whether or not their part of the many millions of dollars spent collectively on various aspects of lake use for commercial purposes, public health, restoration, recreation, science, and maintenance had made any measurable difference in any aspect of the lake over time. None of them had established baseline conditions and committed to periodic re-measurement to see if they were making any progress in whatever their stated mission was with respect to the lake.

This is hardly a unique situation. There are many places in which the complete absence of measurement promotes lack of accountability and results in wasted opportunities to learn how to do the job more effectively. If you work in or are affected by an organization that does no measurement, this book may help you think about how to introduce the concept in a non-threatening and productive way.

When organizations do measure, they tend to measure activities, not outcomes. For example, they may measure how many meetings were held or how many people attended those meetings or how many times the phone rang, or how many comments were received on a report, but rarely do they tie these activities back to any measurement of impact. At the end of the day, who cares how many meetings you held? Does it really matter how many people showed up? Why were you holding the meeting to begin with? What were you trying to accomplish (besides planning another meeting)? It is relatively easy to count activities; it takes more work to figure out how to connect them to outcomes. I believe, and the work I have done with groups all over the country has demonstrated, that we can change this by introducing a participatory and engaging process for measuring progress toward outcomes that helps people make progress together.

Given the serious conditions of economic and political inequality, global warming, species extinction, pandemics, armed conflicts, migrating populations, and more, we can no longer afford these wasteful approaches. We cannot afford waste; we cannot afford to ignore the consequences of our actions and we should not continue to ignore the power of integrating measurement into our work from the start. Measuring results as an afterthought is another all-too-common practice that illustrates an enormous, missed opportunity.

We need to encourage people to think and learn together, not simply follow directions. We need to encourage people to think about the information they really need to make better decisions; not distort their sense of reality by insisting that they use data that is neither relevant nor revealing. We need to be measuring the right things, in the right ways, for the right reasons. Instead, all too often we fail to measure entirely, or we measure the wrong things. Often our measurement processes are extractive and too costly for what we get, and the way in which we use (or fail to use) the information we collect is not conducive to shared learning or continuous improvement.

Individuals and organizations committed to social change are most often supported by what we call 'soft' money; that is philanthropic dollars or public funds that are not tied to the market for goods and services.[1] These entities, be they foundations, private philanthropic funders, or public agencies, typically require various types of reporting from those whom they fund, generally for the purpose of verifying compliance with the terms of the grant.

At a meeting at the Ford Foundation that included representatives of several non-profit organizations working in the field of international development, I was struck by the discussion of the number of staff they support whose only function is to respond to data requests from funders. These staff do nothing to directly contribute to advancing their organizations' missions, nor is it clear to grantees that funding organizations do anything useful to the mission with the data these staff put together for them. It is extremely rare that funders provide actionable insights back to those they support based on the data they extract from grantees. Nor do funders generally engage their grantees in identifying the measures that would be most useful to the grantees' own work on the ground. Instead, funders typically impose a set of measures from the outside. The cost in personnel, energy, and divided focus is enormous.

On top of that, the very thought of measuring performance is often viewed by funding recipients as a threat rather than as an opportunity to learn and improve. This is especially true when measurement requirements are imposed by outsiders to the systems one is trying to impact. All too often, the people doing the actual work on the ground are unable to shape the measures or determine how the results of measurement are used. If they are required to use scarce resources to report on metrics chosen by outsiders that are irrelevant or misleading and against which their own worth is judged, there is every reason to be wary of measurements. If the goal of measurement is to learn how to make positive change more effectively, we need new ways of going about it.

Approaches to measurement

I am not the only one who is interested in reforming the way we approach measurement. The past few decades have seen the introduction of several alternative frameworks for measurement and/or evaluation, including, but not limited to: Results-Based Accountability; Sustainable Community Indicators, Success Measures, and Collective Impact Assessment. Each is based on a somewhat different premise and aimed at somewhat different audiences. I have briefly described these approaches below, highlighting what I consider to be their positive aspects and identifying their limitations. I do not offer these descriptions as a full-blown critique but rather as a way of helping the reader differentiate between these various alternatives and You Get What You Measure (YGWYM), the approach to measurement that is the subject of this volume. The reader is encouraged to learn more about these alternative approaches and judge for themselves.

Results-based accountability

Results-Based Accountability™ (also known as Outcomes Based Accountability in the UK), is an approach developed by Mark Friedman and popularized in his 2009 book *Trying Hard is Not Good Enough* (see also Clear Impact, 2021). Clear Impact is the organization with exclusive and worldwide rights to use Results-Based Accountability (RBA). They describe it as 'a data driven, decision-making process to help communities and organizations get beyond talking about problems to taking action to solve problems'. In my professional experience, getting to action is not the problem. The problem, rather, is too much action without adequate testing of key assumptions, identification of leverage points, or reflection.

RBA claims to be different from all other frameworks because it makes a distinction between population and performance accountability. Population accountability is used with communities to promote community well-being while performance accountability is used with organizations to determine whether customers are better off as a result of services received. It is not clear whether this amounts to two different approaches or is essentially the same approach applied in two different contexts. To their credit, RBA promoters recognize that a single programme, agency, or service system cannot take sole credit for achieving any given 'end' unless that 'end' is extremely narrowly defined.

RBA does a good job of defining 'ends' as conditions of well-being for children, families, and communities as a whole and avoids the trap of 'ends' as activities. However, the approach falls apart after that because it moves directly from 'ends' to choosing an indicator without providing any replicable process to inform the choice. It ignores the wide spectrum of meanings that different stakeholders assign to the desired 'ends'. RBA also makes no distinction between indicators and measures, thus missing out on one of the most powerful steps in creating a shared language of progress.

The State of Vermont adopted RBA in 2013. Michael McCarthy, a newly elected legislator from Franklin County, Vermont, described the experience this way:

> The first training we received in RBA made it clear that we should know the questions we're asking, know the problem we are trying to solve, figure out what information we need, who we should be talking to and how we are going to measure success. It sounded great! These guiding questions appeared on the wall of every conference room in the State House.
>
> I was on the House Transportation Committee. A decade ago, we had terrible pavement conditions. The Agency of Transportation did not have a good inventory of road conditions. As a result of RBA, they started an asset management system that included documenting and recording road conditions. The focus shifted from a life cycle pavement maintenance plan, where every road received attention when it deteriorated, to a prevention plan focused on maintaining good roads. The percentage of roads in poor condition has trended down and the percentage of good condition roads has trended up. This was a pretty easy application of RBA and we could see the curve bend over time.
>
> Where RBA gets really hard is where we spend over half our money, on human services. With human services, it can be very difficult to get everyone on a committee or in a legislature to agree about the problem we are trying to solve or what we are trying to achieve. Often any policy is not just a budget compromise, but a goal compromise. People come with their own agendas to do something or to stop something from being done. They are not starting with genuine curiosity about the issue. The system isn't set up to ask, 'What are we trying to achieve?' or to encourage us to rely on data instead of relying on anecdotes. It's hard to use RBA to decide what your political priorities are going to be. RBA failed us here. Now, because of this, everyone rolls their eyes when people say 'RBA'.
>
> Now we have a Government Accountability Committee that grew out of peoples' frustration with RBA. Because of RBA, there is a genuine desire to find measures that tell us a story and will inform the next year of policy, but it feels like, with certain things like childcare, the investments we would have to make to really make a difference are so big it's almost impossible to make progress.[2]

RBA seems most applicable to situations in which goals are already clear and widely shared and results are concrete and easy to measure using existing metrics. It does not address the issues of developing shared goals, integrating diverse perspectives on how to achieve them, and designing measures of behavioural change that are context specific.

Guide to sustainable community indicators

The *Guide to Sustainable Community Indicators*, authored by Maureen Hart and promoted since around 1995 and updated in 1999, is based on the concept of sustainability indicators as reflections of the interconnectedness of the environment, the economy, and society. The approach to sustainability presented in the Guide is intended for use in community development. It contrasts sustainable indicators with traditional indicators that focus on either the environment, the economy, or society but do not focus on the interconnections between them. The Guide offers a compendium of indicators being used by communities of all sizes and is arranged by topics common to many community development efforts such as business, production, recreation, land use, and transportation.

Some, though not all, sustainable indicators focus on a positive vision for the future, such as the number of students trained for jobs that are available in the local economy versus a more traditional 'indicator' such as the unemployment rate. While Hart emphasizes the importance of selecting indicators for which data is accessible, she also warns against relying exclusively on traditional data sources and suggests that new data sources will need to be developed to truly measure sustainability.

Hart explains the characteristics of effective indicators as relevant, easy to understand, reliable, and based on accessible data, but she does not provide a values-based system for coming up with relevant indicators in context. The Sustainable Community Indicators approach promotes adoption and use of indicators developed elsewhere, primarily by tapping into existing public and/or secondary data sources. Also, like RBA, the Sustainable Community Indicators approach fails to clearly distinguish between indicators of progress and measures.

Success measures

Success Measures is a 'social enterprise' (i.e. consulting service) based at the non-profit organization NeighborWorks, providing guidance in outcome evaluation. It is intended for use by non-profit organizations and their partners active in community development and health-related programming and strategy implementation. Success Measures focuses on giving its clients 'the skills and tools they need to demonstrate results and communicate success'. While the emphasis on 'success' is undoubtedly attractive to potential clients, it may also cause participants to overlook failures and/or neglect to explore assumptions that may be incorrect. For example, if an organization succeeds at expanding internet connections to households with school-age children, because it assumes that lack of reliable connectivity is the number one obstacle to improving access to and benefits from educational programming, it may not pay attention to actual variations in educational attainment once internet is available. The result may be a failure to address equally pertinent issues such as lack of quiet space or nutrition, among others.

Success Measures offers consulting and technical assistance in planning and design, implementation, analysis, reporting, and communicating results. It works with clients to learn how to collect and analyse data using more than 250 ready-to-use data collection tools across relevant content areas related to community development and health. It also allows clients to customize tools to meet the needs of their own programmes. Clients can enter their data, save it, and use it to produce reports. The Success Measures Data System includes integrated survey capability that captures and organizes responses to surveys generated by clients. Surveys are not a particularly valid method for determining existing conditions for reasons discussed in Chapter Nine. Surveys tend to incorporate many untested assumptions about how questions are interpreted by the respondents. However, Success Measures' emphasis on participatory approaches to designing and implementing outcome evaluations that engage community members as well as organizational staff is certainly a step in the right direction (NeighborWorks America, n.d.).

Collective impact

The concept of collective impact supported to achieve large-scale social change was first introduced in a 2011 article by John Kania and Mark Kramer in the *Stanford Social Innovation Review*. This article, targeted to non-profit organizations and funders, highlighted a model for social change supported by a centralized infrastructure ('backbone organization') with dedicated staff and a structured process that leads to a common agenda, shared measurement, continuous communication and mutually reinforcing activities among diverse types of organizations across sectors that share common aspirations. Collective Impact (CI) is contrasted with isolated impact in which funders choose to support individual organizations, no single one of which will ever be able to solve complex social problems at scale on its own.

The authors also argue for a flexible approach to measurement and evaluation based on the complexity and uncertainty surrounding efforts to solve significant social problems, and they highlight the importance of digesting and interpreting the results of measurement before making recommendations. They recognize that the traditional approach where funders hold individual organizations accountable for programme implementation (but not outcomes) is not going to get us where we need to be.

FSG (a consulting firm co-founded by Kramer and Kania) has joined with the Aspen Institute Forum for Community Solutions to form the CI Forum and together they have published a three-part *Guide to Evaluating Collective Impact* (Preskill et al., n.d.). In some respects, the vision of CI and how to evaluate it, as represented in the Guidebook, is aligned with YGWYM. For example, the Guidebook recognizes the importance of continuous learning, or learning for the sake of improved effectiveness, to ensure success in collaborative efforts; it suggests a structure for sharing learning on an ongoing basis; and it argues for using data in the service of learning and accountability[3] by incorporating measurement at the start, not as an afterthought.

However, there are also significant differences. The implementation and evaluation of CI requires a significant investment in a 'backbone organization'. While coordination is essential in working on large-scale systems change, making a separate coordinating organization a prerequisite for learning how to think differently about measurement, outcomes, and how we work together to achieve them limits participation to those non-profits and their partners with the resources required to support such an organization.

CI does not clearly distinguish between goals, outcomes, and activities. It defines outcomes in the short and long term and only its long-term outcomes produce 'changes in condition' (Preskill et al., 2014: 9). As a result, many of the short-term outcomes and indicators recommended in this approach are about knowledge, understandings, and attitudes related to the establishment of a measurement system itself and not the societal change that is the goal. For example, one suggested outcome is '*An effective backbone infrastructure has been identified or established*', for which one suggested indicator of 'early performance' is '*BB staff are respected by important partners and external stakeholders*'. Another example related to mutually reinforcing activities has an outcome stated as, '*Partners have reallocated resources to their highest and best use in support of the CI initiative*', and the recommended indicator is, '*Partners' individual activities are changing to better align with the plan of action*'. Both examples relate to the infrastructure of the CI initiative and embody the assumption that such an infrastructure is necessary to achieve meaningful long-term outcomes.

In contrast, YGWYM may be used by anyone at multiple scales without significant upfront investment and has, over time, led to examples of CI that have grown from the ground up because of the identification of shared goals, key leverage indicators, and a shared language for measurement.

The CI approach relies heavily on 'strategic questions' rather than systems analysis. Beyond a series of guiding questions, CI does not offer a process for determining which indicators are most important or how the measurement of these indicators can be tied directly back to the goal and to specific actions taken to make progress toward it.

In terms of actual measurement, the CI approach uses different types of evaluation during different phases of an initiative, beginning with 'developmental evaluation' then 'formative evaluation', and finally 'summative evaluation'. This assumes that an initiative will last for many years and that 'what works' will not be clear until significant time has elapsed. YGWYM also emphasizes the need for realistic time frames for re-measurement. In the CI world, key 'success factors' in the first 12 to 18 months include a shared understanding of the problem, but not a shared understanding of the condition the initiative is trying to achieve with respect to the problem.

YGWYM recognizes the importance of thinking through the time frame within which observable change might be expected for each measure; it does not suggest three different approaches to evaluation. Instead of setting up performance measures of inputs and outputs in the developmental phase, YGWYM uses participatory systems analysis to determine what the desired condition is at the outset and uses measures to show progress toward goals. The question of 'what difference did it make?' (summative evaluation) is answered in an ongoing way based on context.

I would argue that the initial focus on developmental evaluation or evaluation based on process instead of goals used as 'baby steps' toward better communication among partners in CI initiatives is just as likely to lead to a reinforced sense of business as usual; no one needs to change what they are doing, they just need to share their information with their partners. This appears from the outside to be exactly where many groups using the CI approach get stuck.

The CI approach assumes that funders will continue to require conventional measures of accountability (though becoming friendlier to funding CI initiatives overall). YGWYM strives to change the balance of power in measurement and evaluation from a funder-centric to an integrated approach in which measures are developed by and with practitioners and designed to answer the questions that practitioners need to have answered. This paves the way to more quickly and effectively achieve desired goals shared by practitioners, funders, and supporters.

Measurement for certifications

In addition to social and community development-oriented measurement approaches described above, there are also many different types of certification processes that rely on measurements, from Leadership in Energy and Environmental Design (LEED) to Forest Stewardship, to the International Organization for Standardization (ISO). These programmes apply the same criteria to many different circumstances in an attempt to measure compliance. Since it is extremely difficult to compare things like 'impact on the environment' or 'community contribution' across different management regimes, sectors, designs, geographies, and cultures, much is often lost in translation. Certification processes such as these typically rely on third party verification with its attendant costs. While YGWYM can contribute to a culture of accountability, that is not its primary purpose. It does not require third party verification though it can be adapted to do so if appropriate. Measuring compliance with a fixed set of industry standards is not the focus of the approach introduced in this book.

Balanced scorecards

There are many types of 'scorecards' in use today and many, but by no means all, are based on the balanced scorecard approach. The balanced scorecard is essentially a tool used by business managers to keep track of financial performance in relationship to a business's strategic goals. The balanced scorecard was developed to help businesses connect their short-term financial results to longer-term strategies and relate strategic actions to financial impacts. The measures included in balanced scorecards are designed to show overall trends as well as the impacts of specific business-related initiatives, such as implementing a new IT system. Measures are exclusively quantitative and relate to revenue, costs, operating expenses, marketing performance, and so on.

Strategic goals, called 'strategic objectives', are generally set by top management and executed by those below. They are defined as actions not conditions, they are expected to matter in the medium to long term, and they are constrained by ease of measurement. Relying on ease of measurement generally means sticking to well-established units of measure and data regardless of whether it gives us the information we really need to make better decisions. It also means avoiding 'messy' concepts such as 'aptitude' or 'willingness' or 'satisfaction' that require work to define in measurable terms. 'Some things are just too difficult to quantify. These things are bad candidates for strategic objectives' (Spider Strategies, 2023). This is in direct contrast to the YGWYM approach which encourages creativity in measurement and provides workable approaches to developing measures for 'messy' concepts.

While balanced scorecards and related software can provide a means to manage and track financial data over time, it is not designed to address more complex goals and strategies related to social change, which require the capacity to measure things that are not necessarily quantitative by nature.

Dashboards

Dashboards are essentially ways to display the results of measurement. Depending on how they are set up they may be dynamic and updated in real time or they may be static. Dashboards may present quantitative as well as qualitative data and may allow the user to drill down to underlying data sources and supporting information. Dashboards are not a measurement process; they are a tool for sharing the results of measurement.

Farm to Institution New England (n.d.) provides one example of a dashboard developed in relation to a complex social change strategy. It provides clear information on the sources of underlying data and other related resources. Because each social change initiative is different, the YGWYM process does not include a generic dashboard tool for users, but users may choose to develop their own dashboard to display the results of YGWYM over time.

Conclusion

While each of the above approaches may be used to create positive change, none is focused specifically on helping diverse groups of people think and act together to identify, measure, and make progress toward shared goals regardless of the nature of the goals they would like to achieve or the organizational structure within which they operate. YGWYM offers an alternative strategic approach that invites ongoing participation by diverse stakeholders who learn together as they go. YGWYM grew out of my dissatisfaction with other available methods for strategic planning, including but by no means limited to: analyses of strengths, weaknesses, opportunities, and threats (SWOT), logic models, and brainstorming followed by voting with dots. I have found that while these methods may be useful in certain circumstances, by and large they do not foster the deep collective thinking, or the testing of assumptions required to understand systems and define leverage points for change.

The experience of the YGWYM process brings stakeholders into new relationships with one another, breaks down silos, develops a shared sense of the larger system in which all stakeholders operate, and provides a shared language for ongoing communication. By the time a group of stakeholders has completed the YGWYM process, they know what to do, why they are doing it, and who they need to do it with to make a difference at scale. They also know how to tell whether or not it is working. They have learned how to think strategically and how to focus on what matters and they have agreed on what positive behaviour change would look like.

YGWYM has been used successfully with groups of diverse stakeholders throughout the United States working on social change. It has also been used in Canada and incorporated into work in developing countries. YGWYM has been used to develop shared approaches to sectoral development, organizational development, community development, economic development, and business with robust results.

YGWYM has been applied to topics as diverse as managing the risk of wildfire, farmland preservation, environmental impacts of alternative approaches to energy generation, the challenges of an ageing population, redesigning food systems, expanding markets in forestry and wood products, integrating social determinants of health into community health and wellness efforts, arts and culture, and more. Participants in YGWYM sessions typically appreciate the new insights they gain into how to understand a system and identify key leverage points as well as the chance to interact with a variety of people who have different outlooks and concerns but with whom they can find common ground with the desire to achieve a shared goal.

How to use this book

This book contains much of the information provided in a course I have developed and taught to business, community, academic, and non-profit organizations over the past 15+ years called Becoming a Measurement Guide (BMG). Measurement Guides are the facilitators of the YGWYM process. BMG was designed to help people who are already skilled facilitators learn how to use YGWYM in their work. Therefore, the materials in this book assume a level of skill and familiarity in basic facilitation and facilitation techniques.

This book explains the rationale behind YGWYM and includes tools, exercises, and handouts required to implement it. Readers can treat this book as a primer for how to become a Measurement Guide. The text is supported by selections from a videotaped session of BMG training made in 2012 and edited to correspond to the chapters in the book (see appendix 3).

Engaging participants

As a Measurement Guide, you may recognize situations where the YGWYM process would be beneficial before others recognize it. As one Measurement Guide put it, 'I see opportunities to use YGWYM every time I turn around, but people just don't. They are in the habit of doing it the way they do it. They can't see the opportunities.'[4] Whenever you see groups or organizations struggling to come to consensus, unclear about their goals, rushing to actions based on untested assumptions, working at cross purposes, or failing to include relevant stakeholders in the conversation, it is likely that they could benefit from the YGWYM process. They are doing the best they can, but they do not have the right tools. Part of your job as a Measurement Guide is to build enough trust to enable participants to take the first step along the YGWYM journey. We have found that stakeholders respond positively to invitations to YGWYM sessions that emphasize the opportunity to engage with a wide variety of stakeholders to learn about an issue that matters to the recipient. After participating in the initial session, personal investment in the process drives ongoing participation.

Before you begin your work with any specific group, you will want to familiarize yourself with the entirety of the YGWYM process. While it is important not to skip any part of the process to get to another, some groups may find great benefit in early stages of the process even without completing the entire process. Measurement Guides, in consultation with their clients, determine how much of the YGWYM process groups are ready to undertake at any given time. Some groups may focus only on goals. Others may go beyond that to indicators and an indicator analysis. Others may be ready to move to measures, measurement plans, and actions. The YGWYM process is content neutral; every group brings their own content to it.

The YGWYM process can be delivered in a series of sessions, on consecutive days or spread out over time. We recommend allowing at least half a day per session to allow time for deep listening and for relationships to develop among stakeholders. The Measurement Guide must trust the process and convey that trust to participants, encouraging them to stick with it and avoid skipping steps. Measurement Guides prevent groups from reverting to more familiar processes so that participants can discover the power of this process for themselves. For most, the YGWYM process will be qualitatively different from other group planning processes in which they have participated. Participants may be justifiably sceptical to start; in our experience that scepticism melts the further they go in the process.

The YGWYM process is highly interactive and its success depends, in part, on making sure that all participants are heard and engaged. Toward this end, we recommend a minimum of one trained Measurement Guide for every 30 participants if the process is conducted face to face, and one Measurement Guide per breakout room if it is conducted digitally. We have successfully used the process with groups of 100 or more at one time.

When working with more than 10–12 participants, it is best to divide the group into tables or breakout rooms of no more than 10–12 (or even fewer). This is especially important during the indicator analysis. Each table or breakout room should contain a variety of different types of stakeholders.

We also recommend that you evaluate each session to get a sense of what participants are taking away. Figure 1.1 presents a basic evaluation form that you should feel free to adapt to your own needs.

Finally, in keeping with the spirit of engagement and personal responsibility that underlies the YGWYM approach, we recommend allowing participants to establish their own ground rules. We do this by first acknowledging that participants have likely been in many workshops or working group sessions over the course of their lives. Then we ask them two questions (see Figure 1.2):

1. Think of the most productive group working sessions you have ever been a part of. What are the behaviours of yourself and others that made them so good?
2. Now think of the worst. What are the behaviours of yourself and others that made them so bad?

We make a list of responses to each question, noting duplications, and then we suggest that this working session will go best if everyone avoids the negative behaviours and strives for the positive behaviours. This places the responsibility on participants and empowers them to enforce productive behaviours among each other.[5]

Materials and exercises

This book is organized according to the way in which the YGWYM process unfolds. Each chapter introduces and illustrates key concepts. Some chapters provide links to video clips of an actual Becoming a Measurement Guide training session. Worksheets and related materials are included where relevant.

Materials included in this book include:

- Exercises that are fundamental to and required by the YGWYM process. Exercises are embedded in the text and include instructions for Measurement Guides (facilitators).
- Worksheets we use with YGWYM participants. These may be copied and used as needed.
- In addition, portions of all chapters in this book are supported by YouTube videos of a Becoming a Measurement Guide course recorded in 2012.

You Get What You Measure

Workshop Evaluation
Session Name, Date

1) What did you like best about this workshop?

2) What did you like least?

3) How would you rate the overall effectiveness of the workshop facilitation?
              Not at All   Very
                    1   2   3   4   5

4) How would you rate the effectiveness of the activities and exercises used during this workshop?
              Not at All   Very
                    1   2   3   4   5

5) How and with whom will you use what you've learned in this workshop over the next six months?

6) Would your ecommend this workshop to others?

7) Your suggestions for improving this workshop:

Figure 1.1 Sample workshop evaluation form
Source: © Yellow Wood Associates, Inc.

Background reading

We also recommend the following background reading for Measurement Guides: *Leverage Points: Places to Intervene in a System*, by Donella Meadows;[6] *Emerging Issues in Learning Communities*, written for the Appalachian Regional

You Get What You Measure

Worksheet

Creating our own ground rules

Think of the most productive group working sessions you have ever been a part of:

What are the behaviours that made them so good?

Now think of the worst:

What are the behaviours that made them so bad?

Figure 1.2 Creating our own ground rules worksheet
Source: © Yellow Wood Associates, Inc.

Commission by Shanna Ratner;[7] and *Strengthening Rural Families – By the Numbers: Using Data to Drive Action on Behalf of Children and Families* by Betsy Rubiner for the Annie E. Casey Foundation.[8] Though these were written several years ago, their content remains quite relevant today. They provide additional background and insights into some of the thinking behind the YGWYM process.

Notes

1. Except insofar as they derive, in the case of philanthropy, from excess income often originally earned through some type of market-based

activity that has been invested to become a stock of wealth, and, for public funding, from taxes on earned income as well as unearned income.

2. Personal communication with Michael McCarthy, 18 November 2019, St Albans, VT.

3. Accountability is a nuanced concept in the context of collective action. It includes accountability to collaborating partners, accountability to collect and use data in decision-making, and accountability to a common agenda.

4. Barbara Wyckoff, trained Measurement Guide, interview with author, 11 December 2019.

5. This exercise also provides an opportunity to address the people who think that the success of a workshop is entirely the responsibility of the facilitator by pointing out that: 1) there is one facilitator and however many participants; and 2) this is a highly participatory workshop and everyone needs to engage productively to make the process valuable for all of us.

6. <http://donellameadows.org/archives/leverage-points-places-to-intervene-in-a-system/> [accessed 3 October 2020].

7. <https://www.yellowwood.org/emerging-issues-for-learning-communities.html> [accessed 15 March 2020].

8. aecf.org/resources/strengthening-rural-families [accessed 29 August 2020].

References

Aspen Institute Rural Economic Policy Program (1996) *Measuring Community Capacity Building: A Workbook in Progress for Rural Communities*, The Aspen Institute, Washington, DC.

Clear Impact (no date) 'What is results-based accountability™?' [online] <https://clearimpact.com/results-based-accountability/> [accessed 3 January 2021].

Farm to Institution New England (no date) Metrics dashboard. <http://dashboard.farmtoinstitution.org/> [accessed 5 December 2020].

Friedman, M. (2009) *Trying Hard is Not Good Enough*, BookSurge Publishing.

Hart, M. (1999) *Guide to Sustainable Community Indicators*, ed. II [online], Hart Environmental Data, North Andover, MA.

Kania, J. and Kramer, M. (2011) 'Collective impact', *Stanford Social Innovation Review* Winter 2011: 36–41 <https://doi.org/10.48558/5900-kn19>.

NeighborWorks America (no date) Success Measures [website] <https://successmeasures.org/> [accessed 13 January 2021].

Preskill, H., Parkhurst, M. and Splansky Juster, J. (2014) *Guide to Evaluating Collective Impact 03*, Collective Impact Forum. <https://ncg.org/sites/default/files/resources/Guide%20to%20Evaluating%20CI%2003.pdf> [accessed 6 February 2023].

Preskill, H., Parkhurst, M. and Splansky, J. (no date) *Guide to Evaluating Collective Impact 01* [online], Collective Impact Forum. <https://www.fsg.org/publications/guide-evaluating-collective-impact> [accessed 4 February 2021].

Spider Strategies (2023) What is a balanced scorecard? [online] <https://balancedscorecards.com/balanced-scorecard/#learn-objectives> [accessed 16 January 2023].

CHAPTER 2
Why measure?

We all measure things every day, whether we are conscious of it or not. We pay attention to things like how much food is in the refrigerator, how many dust bunnies have accumulated under the bed or the sofa, how much gas is in the car, what mood our child, spouse, or friend is in and so much more. There are many ways of measuring and only some of them involve instrumentation. We measure when we observe (e.g. how many cars are parked in that restaurant's parking lot?), when we count (e.g. how much money is in my wallet?), when we use an instrument to inform us (e.g. what does the thermometer read this morning?), and when we 'get a sense' (e.g. what mood is my child in?). The point is that there are certain things we each choose to pay attention to and we do it for a reason. The reason has to do with the condition we are trying to achieve or in other words – our goal.

At the beginning of every training in YGWYM, we do an exercise we call Everyday Measurement. In it, we ask participants to write down a few things they measure or pay attention to as part of their personal life. Then we ask them to find a partner and share one of the things they measure along with the decisions or actions they take based on the data they collect. After this exchange, we invite people to share what they or their partner measure and the action they take. Then we ask them *why* they pay attention to that thing in particular. What are they trying to achieve? Some of my favourite exchanges have included these:

> 'I measure the length of the grass. If it's getting too long (over about three inches) I know I have to mow it.'
>
> 'So, the result of your measurement affects your behaviour?'
>
> 'Yes.'
>
> 'OK. Why do you mow the grass? What are you trying to achieve?'
>
> 'Oh, I mow it to keep my wife happy.'
>
> 'So, the real reason you measure the length of the grass is because you want your wife to be happy. That is your goal. Otherwise, the length of the grass wouldn't really matter to you.'
>
> 'That's right.'

Here is another one:

> 'I measure the amount of exercise I get every day.'
>
> 'How do you do that?'

'I keep track of the minutes I spend exercising. I use a watch.'

'What do you do with the information?'

'If I haven't exercised for at least 30 minutes, I make sure to do it before I go to bed.'

'So, the result of your measurement affects your behaviour?'

'Yes.'

'Why do you pay attention to the amount of exercise you get every day? What are you trying to achieve?'

'I want to get 30 minutes of exercise every day.'

'OK, but why?'

'Because when I exercise at least 30 minutes a day I feel better and my joints don't hurt.'

'So, you pay attention to how much you exercise every day because you want to be comfortable in your body?'

'Yes.'

This exercise is powerful in several ways. First, it establishes that measurement is a normal human activity, not something that requires a PhD. Second, it introduces the concept that there are many ways to measure. Third, it establishes the clear connection we make in our own lives between what we pay attention to and *what we do*. Unlike so many organizations and bureaucracies, as individuals we generally do not measure just for the sake of measuring. The information we get from measuring *informs our behaviour*. And finally, it illustrates that there is *always* some implicit goal or condition we are trying to achieve that guides what we choose to measure in the first place. When we tease out our implicit goals, we may find better ways to achieve them.

YGWYM strives to integrate measurement into the everyday life of collective efforts to make progress toward shared goals as fully as we integrate measurement into our own everyday lives as individuals. Measurement is a matter of paying attention. What we pay attention to determines the actions we take or do not take. In this way, our attention creates our reality. We do, in fact, get what we measure. The everyday measurement worksheet in Figure 2.1 is the tool we use for this exercise.

Precision in measurement

Some measures are more precise than others. A measure need be only as precise as necessary to inform our decisions and our actions. Sometimes that requires being correct to the tenth decimal place; more often it does not. One of my favourite stories that speaks to this point is the story of a group of citizens who were concerned about the impact of a factory located upstream from their community on the water quality in the river near their homes. They had long noticed that the river became cloudy every time the factory

Worksheet
Everyday measurement

1) Using the space below, take three minutes to list as many things as you can that you count or measure as part of your daily life (not connected to work).

2) Share your work with those at your table by having each participant pick one measurement off their list and describe what kinds of decisions or actions they take based upon the measurement.

What I measure:

_____

_____

_____

_____

_____

_____

_____

_____

_____

_____

_____

Figure 2.1 Everyday measurement worksheet

discharged material into it. They had complained about this to the proper authorities, but no one took them seriously. They decided that they needed evidence. But they were just a group of citizens, not scientists. They did not have scientific equipment or access to a laboratory to analyse water samples. So, what could they do? They decided to invest in white sneakers. They chose a spot on the bank of the river and measured the number of steps into the water toward the middle of the river they could take before they could no longer see their white sneakers. They conducted this experiment and carefully recorded the information every day for some period of time; long enough to establish a pattern. Then they obtained information on the dates and times of the factory releases of effluent. They determined there was a direct correlation between the factory releases and increased turbidity (cloudiness) in the river. They took this data to state authorities and the authorities finally took them seriously enough to begin their own, more scientific, testing procedures.

I love this story, not only because it speaks to the question of degrees of precision in measurement and the power of approximation, but also because it clearly illustrates that measurement can be a creative process that draws on our best problem-solving skills. It is also a great reminder that measurement does not necessarily require fancy equipment, but it does require consistent and verifiable protocols. This group had to conduct their experiment at the same place and the same times of day using the same tools (white sneakers and a yardstick for depth) and the same unit of measure (i.e. the number of steps into the river until they could no longer see their sneakers and depth of the river at that point) over a period of time.

How the process of measurement helps us learn

We have already seen that we measure in our own lives because we wish to make progress toward certain conditions or goals. In the example above, the group chose to measure to verify their casual observations and be able to share the results with others who could take action to help the group achieve its goal of reducing turbidity or cloudiness in the river. Measurement allowed them to test their assumption that there was a direct correlation between upstream discharges and downstream turbidity. In this instance, the results confirmed their assumption. Had the results been otherwise, it would have given them reason to ask more questions and reassess their assumption. Perhaps there were other things causing the turbidity that also would have to be addressed.

Testing assumptions

Testing our individual and collective assumptions is one of the important reasons to measure. We all make assumptions all the time. We must make assumptions because we do not have the capacity to know all there is to know. However, when our assumptions are wrong, which is more often than we might care to admit, they limit our sense of what is possible. The act of measuring can help us reshape our understanding of the world, what is possible, and how progress can be made. For example, there was a time when everyone assumed the world was flat. That limited interest in exploration because what if you fell off the edge?! Today, many people assume that an unanswered email means the person or organization they wrote to is not interested in what they had to say, and they proceed to write them off. What if the reality was that the sent message never got through or ended up in a spam folder and was never read? Would it still make sense to write off the intended recipient, or would it make more sense to follow up?

At the collective level, what if a community assumes it must rely on external providers to repair its infrastructure when, in fact, the resources to do the work already exist within the community? Often, this assumption leads to indefinite postponement of needed upgrades because the cost of relying on external contractors can be quite high. This results in frustration, disempowerment, and ongoing resource degradation. On the other hand, when the assumption is tested, it can reveal a host of other alternatives. For example, the Rensselaerville Institute ran a self-help water and wastewater programme for small towns for many years. This enabled small communities to address water and wastewater deficiencies effectively and safely without incurring the high costs of professional contractors by using local equipment, expertise, and volunteers (Schautz and Conway, 2016). Requirements regarding health and safety were met in cooperation with local and state authorities. In my own town of Fairfield, Vermont, the Selectboard put a project out for bid in 2019 to professional design and engineering firms to rebuild a sand shed. Responses ranged from $720,000 to $1.1 m. Instead of accepting a bid, they decided to have the local road crew do the work itself with some volunteer assistance at a cost of $395,000.[1] In each case, a willingness to test a prevailing assumption about the need for external contractors and assess the availability and applicability of local resources changed the actions taken.

To emphasize the self-limiting nature of assumptions, we sometimes ask workshop participants to do an exercise we call Everyday Assumptions. It begins by asking participants to reflect on and write down one or two assumptions that may govern their behaviour in their personal or professional lives. Next, we ask them to imagine how the world would look different if their assumptions were incorrect. Finally, we ask them to think of one thing they might do to test their assumptions. At a recent workshop, one participant shared her assumption that coming into work no later than 9 a.m. set a good example for her co-workers. However, as the group probed further, we discovered that she was expected to be in at 8 a.m. but often worked well past 5 p.m. so she had adjusted her own start time to compensate. Since she had not shared her thinking with her co-workers, it is entirely possible that they interpreted her behaviour in the opposite way from what she intended! She could test her assumption by speaking with and observing the work schedules of her co-workers.

In the example above about measuring the length of the grass to keep his wife happy, once we uncovered the goal, it became clear to the participant that there might actually be other things even more important than keeping the grass cut that he could be paying attention to in pursuit of the goal. He left the workshop committed to testing his assumption about the relative importance of mowing the lawn! (See Chapter Six for Everyday Assumptions Worksheet.)

Fuelling continuous learning through reflection

We are blessed as human beings with the capacity to learn. Confucius tells us, 'By three methods we may learn wisdom: First, by reflection, which is noblest; Second, by imitation, which is easiest; and third, by experience, which is the bitterest.'

We live in a culture that is long on action or experience (just do it) and imitation (repeating what others have done). We spend most of our time doing and very little of our time trying to understand the impacts of what we have done (reflection). This is true for us as individuals as well as within our organizations. Unfortunately, accumulating experiences and/or imitating the actions of others do not maximize our capacity for learning. Reflection, or the time spent articulating and codifying our experience, figuring out what we actually did in relation to what we were trying to do, is a crucial component of learning (Di Stefano et al., 2014, 2015, 2016). Without taking time for reflection, we lose the chance to figure out how to improve our performance, individually and collectively.

Our tendency is often to do the same things over and over again, yet, as the saying goes, 'If you keep on doing what you're doing, you will keep on getting what you've got.' We are most comfortable doing what we know how to do. Doing things differently can be uncomfortable and even frightening. Many of us have a strong preference to stay within our 'comfort zones'. To make matters worse, the systems we work within, including the incentive structures we respond to, often dictate that we do things that do not make sense in relationship to the goals we are trying to achieve, but 'it's the way things are done around here', or 'it's the way we've always done it'. However, our lack of reflection means that we are often working hard but not working smart. Rarely do we even clearly articulate our goal or the condition we are trying to achieve. This tendency is aptly summarized by another popular expression, 'If you don't know where you're going, any road will get you there'.

When we embed the process of measurement and re-measurement into our individual and collective work, we build in content (the results of measurement) and a process for interpreting the content that requires the ongoing reflection that is so critical to learning. The process of measurement helps us focus by requiring us to articulate our goals. It provides discipline by forcing us to define our actions in relation to our goals. It requires us to measure baseline conditions *before* we act and on an ongoing basis thereafter so that we can tell whether or not we are making progress. It helps us identify what we know and *what we don't know* about the system we are working within before we try to change it. Reflection allows us to learn and discover the changes we need to make to get better at what we do, to change the systems in which we operate, and to move toward the goals we want to achieve. Reflection and the time it requires is not a luxury; it is a necessity if we are to learn how to get better at solving the many problems that confront us as a society. Time spent reflecting often results in more effective action especially when we reflect together.

Information flow

As Donella Meadows wrote, 'Missing feedback is one of the most common causes of systems malfunction'.[2] Systems are highly sensitive to the ways in which information flows through them because flows of information create feedback loops and feedback loops inform our behaviour. For example, households that have an electricity meter installed where they can see it on a daily basis are more likely to conserve electricity than those who have no convenient way of getting information about the amount of electricity they are using in real time. When no information is available, there is no feedback loop except perhaps a monthly bill and the lag time is often too great to affect behaviour. Information that flows in a timely manner and is accessible to the people whose behaviour affects the system directly can change the way the system operates and the results it achieves.

Often, information is not readily available to those who need it. Several years ago, a town in Maine had beaches that were regularly closed by the State due to environmental contamination. The community prioritized re-opening their beaches as a key to community sustainability. Before they could act, they needed to know exactly what they were dealing with. Which contaminants were a problem at which beaches? So, they contacted the Maine Department of Environmental Protection and asked for the information they needed. They were told that, although the data was collected on a beach-by-beach basis, once it was inputted into the computer system, there was no way to extract it on that basis. Instead of giving up, the community kept asking questions until they were connected directly with the staff person managing the relevant database. Once they explained what they were after and why, that staff person took the initiative to get them what they needed. By identifying and winning over the information gatekeeper, they were able to inform themselves of the baseline conditions of their beaches and develop targeted strategies to clean them up. Once they had built the relationship, they could go back for data over time and measure the impact of their actions, creating a feedback loop where none had previously existed.

Too many of our information systems are extractive; designed to move information from actors close to the ground to those further away without provisions to bring the information back to the ground in an accessible and timely manner. Without adequate feedback loops, people who seek to change systems are flying blind. The first way the measurement process changes patterns of information flow and lays the groundwork for systems change is by identifying the specific information needed to create the feedback loops that will help the system move toward the desired goals. Sometimes, as in the case of the Maine beaches, the information already exists but it is not getting to the people who need it in a timely and accessible way. In other instances, the information may not exist in a useful form. For example, suppose a community wishes to be sure that every resident has adequate nutrition. A food bank serves certain residents, a Meals on Wheels programme serves others, and the school offers free and reduced cost meals to yet another group. However, no one has consistent information about the nutritional status of all residents. In this instance, establishing a baseline can create new information *and* new information flows between and among multiple stakeholders.

The second way in which the process of YGWYM changes patterns of information flow and lays the groundwork for systems change has to do with the broad group of stakeholders brought together to engage in the measurement process. We recommend engaging three kinds of stakeholders from the start:

- People and organizations that need to be involved to make progress toward the shared goal. Think of this as the 'take action' category.
- People and organizations that can prevent progress toward the shared goal. Think of this as the 'stop action' category.
- People who are likely to be affected by actions taken to make progress toward the shared goal. Think of this as the 'impacted by action' category.

Generally, no matter what the topic, sector, challenge or concern you would like to address, you have some notions at the outset of at least some of the people or organizations who need to be involved to make progress. This is the first group: the 'take action' category. In our experience, stakeholder engagement in most planning and measurement processes begins and ends with this group. That is a mistake.

It is likely that you will discover a few things about this group as you work your way through the process. First, you may discover that some of the people and organizations that you thought were in the first category are really in the second because they are less open to alternative approaches than you might have imagined. For example, when the Ford Foundation approached well-known economic development organizations in the Deep South with the opportunity to receive funding in exchange for piloting a new approach to economic development, the established organizations were happy to receive funding, but unwilling to change their ways of working. Instead, Ford reached out to less well-known organizations who were more curious and willing to experiment. Second, you may discover that some of the people and organizations you had assumed were influencers are not and that other organizations you had not previously identified really belong at that table. For example, in the many years of work we have done in economic development, we have frequently seen clients, particularly if they are non-profits themselves, begin with the assumption that non-profit organizations were key to their success only to realize that the real movers and shakers in economic development were in the for-profit sector. Often these were individuals and companies with whom non-profits were not in relationship, so inviting them to the table immediately changed the flow of information. Third, you may discover that some of the people or organizations you initially thought would be able to help lack the capacity to make a meaningful contribution or cannot be relied on to do what they say they will do. In any case, you want to involve those whose engagement and support are going to be needed to make progress as you figure out who they really are.

The second group of stakeholders in the 'stop action' category can prevent progress from being made. Their engagement in the process is equally important. Several years ago, we were working with a group in Maine on an economic development project led by a local environmental group. They had an idea for a business incubator to support natural resource-based businesses. We met several times and we were making some progress in determining the feasibility of their idea when a group of industrialists who had not been invited to the table began to promulgate a conspiracy theory regarding the project based on the leadership role of the environmental group. They accused the group of really wanting to impose restrictions on natural resource use. The group was practically derailed by these accusations, as can easily happen when uninformed fears enter the public discourse. Had the environmental group engaged the industrialists at the outset, there is a reasonable chance that the backlash could have been avoided.

The third group, in the 'impacted by action' category, are people who will be affected by progress. They are almost always left out of the early conversation and may be left out of the entire process unless they rise up to challenge it. Yet, it is often the people who will be most affected by the process who are the intended beneficiaries. Inviting representatives of this group in at the beginning allows them to 1) provide invaluable insights into the nature of reality as they experience it; 2) explain and demonstrate how they might be affected by any proposed actions; and 3) help to design actions that are most likely to have the desired effects without generating negative unintended consequences. As their engagement grows into a sense of ownership, they can become invaluable allies and proponents of the process, but only if their concerns are given voice and addressed in the design phase.

These three categories of stakeholders are neither mutually exclusive nor exhaustive. Some individuals or organizations may fall into multiple categories and may switch categories depending on how the work progresses. Yet, thinking of these three categories of stakeholders at the outset helps embed a wider set of perspectives in the process and often results in unexpected exchanges of information and new patterns of information flow as groups become more familiar with each other's perspectives and priorities and begin to see how they interrelate. Specifically, the measurement process helps diverse stakeholders discover the relationship between self-interest (what matters to each stakeholder), shared interest (how what matters to one stakeholder relates to what matters to others), and common interest (how they wish to make the world a better place regardless of self-interest).

There is great power in bringing these three types of stakeholders together face to face and introducing them to a process that builds relationships, creates commitment to a shared goal, and provides a shared vocabulary to communicate about progress. Often these groups do not have a common vocabulary at the beginning of their interactions. They may use different words to mean the same thing or the same words to mean quite different things. The YGWYM process builds a shared vocabulary that is necessary for making meaningful progress toward shared goals.

In our experience, the best way to get any stakeholder engaged is through a personal invitation that explains why their input is important to the process. Do not be afraid to invite people you do not know or people who have a reputation as disruptors. Simply level with them in advance, explain why you want them there, and let them know that certain behaviours will not be tolerated. Get their agreement to abstain from those behaviours in advance and then hold them to it. While this may feel risky and intimidating the first time you do it, it can be quite effective and is far preferable to either 1) excluding people with potentially valuable perspectives on the basis of their reputations; or 2) allowing bad actors to act out. It never hurts to offer a meal as well, and, if resources permit, a stipend to cover expenses. Often, however, simply the opportunity to meet new types of stakeholders who share an interest in a particular type of social change that matters (or could matter) to the invitee is sufficient to motivate participation.

There is another way to think about stakeholders that can be overlaid on the three groups identified above. Within each group, it may be helpful to think about people who play different roles in social interactions. There are many different typologies that can be used for this. One worth considering in the context of social change work is Malcolm Gladwell's (2000) division of people into 'connectors', 'mavens', and 'salesmen'. 'Connectors' are people specialists. They move between different stakeholder groups and know a lot of different kinds of people. 'Mavens' are information specialists. They are driven to know everything there is to know on a given topic. 'Salesmen' are charismatic and can persuade others to engage. You may not know which of these types you have in the room to start with but paying attention to this over time may help the process become more impactful.

YGWYM can also accommodate content experts. While 'mavens' may be experts on what is going on in a community, content experts possess scientific knowledge and familiarity with research related to the topic at hand. For example, in a YGWYM workshop on preventing catastrophic wildfire in Arizona that included county, state, Native American, and a wide range of non-native community participants, we also invited several people with significant content expertise related to the causes, prevention, and management of wildfires. Their role throughout the workshop was to listen and flag any statements being made that were based on assumptions that ran contrary to scientific knowledge. Periodically, they were given the opportunity to share what they were hearing and inform participants about what they knew. They did not participate directly in any of the exercises, but by listening, flagging, and informing, the entire group was assured that their analyses were based on the best science available. The experts themselves were excited to have this opportunity to listen because it helped them learn more about what other people knew or thought they knew about wildfires.

Capturing the results of experimentation and mitigating risk

Social change work is inherently uncertain and risky. It is always possible that, even with the best of intentions, our actions will make things worse, not better. One of the main ways to address this risk is by paying attention to the impacts we have on the things we are trying to change. If we run an experiment but fail to understand the baseline conditions and what has changed as a result, we cannot learn from it. Measurement provides a process for paying attention that not only helps us know if we are making progress but can also calm fears regarding negative consequences.

The act of measuring or monitoring can play a powerful role in social dynamics as well. Sometimes, the willingness to measure or monitor impacts can convert resistors or sceptics into willing participants. We had just such an experience working with people interested in organizing a canoe trail in the Dragon Run region of Virginia. The Dragon Run is a relatively pristine waterway and those who live on and near it were fearful that a paddling trail would result in an increase in littering along the banks. This concern overwhelmed local support for the enterprise. No amount of verbal reassurance and statements of intent from the proponents would allay their fears. However, when proponents agreed to a monitoring programme that citizens could participate in that would determine whether there was an increase in littering, the flat-out resistance became a kind of curiosity to see what would really happen. Furthermore, proponents agreed that if such an increase was found they would all work together to find ways to address it. Agreeing to measure and share the results built trust among various groups of stakeholders. Ultimately, the group decided to eliminate concern over littering by offering a reservation only experience in which all equipment is provided, including guides.[3] This was the solution to the concern over littering that stakeholders agreed upon as a result of engaging in the YGWYM process.

On a broader level, the act of measuring is a way of attempting to exert control over our unpredictable circumstances, and to establish the basis for predictions. Our desire to control is generally rooted in our fear of the unknown. Fear is a powerful motivator, yet it tends to crowd out curiosity. The YGWYM process works to bring curiosity back into play through measurement.

A note on accountability

Outcomes vs. compliance

The question of accountability is usually posed as, 'Did you do what you said you were going to do?' The focus is on actions taken, not results achieved. Measures are often of inputs, for example, 'did you use the money to buy the supplies you said you would buy?' and outputs, for example, 'how many trainings did you hold and how many people showed up?' While the answers to these questions may be important from a management perspective, they are not the focus of YGWYM. In our experience, measurement tied to account-ability focuses on compliance. YGWYM is more interested in measurement as a means of learning about how to improve outcomes.

We are not interested in measuring inputs and outputs; we are interested in measuring behavioural change that counts as progress toward our goals. We do not care about, say, what supplies you bought if the result was the behavioural change we were looking for. Likewise, we do not care how many trainings you held or how many people attended them; we care about whether the training led to measurable behavioural change that endured over time. If the supplies you bought did not work as planned and the training did not produce the intended results, you should ask 'why not' and 'what will we do differently next time?' How would your resource allocation decisions be different if you were held accountable for outcomes instead of inputs and outputs?

Goodhart's law

The second reason we do not make it a point to use YGWYM to demonstrate accountability has to do with Goodhart's law. Goodhart's law can be expressed as: 'When a measure becomes a target, it ceases to be a good measure' (Koehrsen, 2018: 1). Goodhart's law describes what happens when a person or an organization mistakes a metric for a goal. When metrics are used as narrow targets, and incentive systems are not aligned to outcomes, people will game the targets to benefit themselves. For example, when teachers are told that their own chances for advancement and extra pay are tied to the test scores of their students, in addition to 'teaching to the test' rather than teaching the skills students need to find the answers for themselves, some teachers will actually falsify the test results to gain personal advantage (or avoid the disincentive of being fired). Using measures as targets in this way often leads to unintended, usually negative, consequences. According to David Manheim, an expert on Goodhart's law, it is important not to push too hard for optimization and it helps to rely on people's judgement once goals are understood, instead of attempting to control behaviour by establishing narrow targets (Manheim, 2019). YGWYM keeps the focus on goals and helps improve collective judgement related to what really constitutes progress toward shared goals. The power of YGWYM is not in the measures themselves, but in the process through which they are identified and implemented.

Contribution vs. attribution

Social change is complex, and no single person or organization can change entire systems by themselves. With such complexity, a focus on account-ability is self-limiting. Instead, this process uses measurement to help partners understand the ways in which multiple stakeholders contribute to systems change rather than attributing success to one specific action, organization, or individual.

Supporting self-organizing behaviour

We live in a world that is constantly changing along with our perceptions of it. We need ways to work together to solve emerging problems efficiently and with greater ease, and ideally, in ways that do not require establishing new organizations. Yet we tend to rely on bureaucratic, top-down organizations to solve our problems, and our answer to unsolved problems is often to create yet another organization. Bureaucracies are characterized by hierarchical management with concentrations of power in relatively few hands at the top, with worker bees underneath who are reduced to following orders. Worker bees generally have a limited understanding of the overall intent of the organization they work for, let alone a voice in determining that intent. Bureaucracies are known for excessive red tape and inefficiencies, routine, rigidity, lack of responsiveness, and failure to deliver. This is true of bureaucracies at all levels – international, national, regional, local – and in all sectors – government, non-profit, and for profit. People who work in bureaucracies as well as people who rely on the services provided by bureaucracies are often frustrated. The roots of the word 'bureaucracy' come from combining the French word for desk ('bureau') with '-cratie', a suffix denoting a kind of government. People who spend too much time behind a desk quickly lose touch with the effects of their work on the world outside.

One alternative to top-down or bureaucratic organization is self-organization. Self-organization is a process whereby a range of actors or stakeholders organize themselves around a goal without being directed to do so by an external or governing authority. Margaret Wheatley (1994: 95) writes, 'Self-organization succeeds when the system supports the independent activities of its members by giving them, quite literally, a strong frame of reference.' The force around which self-organizing systems cohere is *meaning* or *purpose*.[4] The process can be spontaneous and result in new systems of interaction based on local resources and creativity, rather than replication of an externally imposed system.

Self-organizing behaviour begins with the recognition of a shared goal or condition that many individuals and groups have a stake in creating. This is the seed around which self-organizing occurs and it provides the focus for networking, coordination, and even collaboration (Himmelman, 2002).

We humans are easily distracted and without a compelling goal to focus on our actions quickly lose connection. In a self-organizing system, each participant finds their own way to contribute to the goal without being told what to do. Each participant draws on their specific talents, resources, and creativity to do the things that they do best, relying on others to do the same. The effects of the actions of a constellation of stakeholders are greater than that of any single actor.

YGWYM supports self-organizing behaviour by allowing diverse groups of stakeholders to articulate shared goals and unpack them to understand what they really mean from a variety of perspectives. Then they go further to define, again from a variety of perspectives, what has to change to make progress toward those goals. Once this understanding is achieved, groups can find their own ways to contribute toward progress in the absence of hierarchical, top-down, centralized control. The use of measures of progress creates the feedback loops that keep actions focused on the goal and support shared learning and adaptivity. This approach can be effective even in otherwise divisive situations.

Back in the 1990s, the State of Oregon was experiencing high and increasing rates of teenage pregnancies. At that time, there was also increasing polarization between abstinence-only advocates and comprehensive sex education proponents. Organizations representing these views not only did not work together, they demonized each other's work. In 2005, the Governor's Office asked an ad hoc committee of state agency representatives and private partners to create a new plan. Rather than try to resolve conflicting philosophies, the committee recognized that all groups had a shared interest in the goal of reducing teenage pregnancies and that any successful approach needed to address youth and families with diverse needs, values, and preferences. In other words, if every group did what they did best, but saw themselves as part of a larger system, they would be able to use their scarce resources to get the job done instead of attempting to hinder each other. This meant, among other things, establishing communication so that if a youth or family came to one organization (e.g. an abortion provider), but desired the services of another (e.g. an adoption agency), these organizations agreed to make referrals to each other (Nystrom et al., 2013). Sex education in Oregon schools includes information about abstinence *and* contraception. This was the beginning of what has become a 20+ year effort resulting in significant decreases in Oregon's teenage pregnancy rates from 48 pregnancies to 32 pregnancies per 1,000 females ages 15–19 years between 2008 and 2012 (Oregon Health Authority, 2015: 7).

Helping us tell our stories

Stories are one of the most powerful ways we have to communicate with each other. Much has been written about the way stories influence our thinking and our behaviour. The psychology of stories suggests they are a primal form of communication that promotes collaboration and connection across geographies and generations. A well-constructed story provides order and grist for how we think and what we think is possible. Stories engage our imaginations in the tasks of empathy and innovation (Rutledge, 2011).

A good story has a beginning, a middle, and an end. The measurement process helps us construct compelling stories by establishing: 1) the beginning – a baseline – our best understanding of the current situation and a goal or the condition we seek to achieve; 2) the middle – a clear articulation of actions we take and how we believe they are related to our goal; and 3) the end – the behavioural changes and measurable impacts that result.

All too often, we do not take the time in our work for social change to create the conditions for powerful storytelling. For example, without taking the time to establish the baseline relevant to our work, we do not know where we began. Stories without a credible baseline begin and often end in the middle – here is what we did. OK, but why did you choose to do that and not something else? What were you trying to achieve? What difference did it make? Too many stories begin and end with action. We fed x number of people or we built y number of houses. So what? How did this affect the overall conditions of hunger or homelessness in your target area?

Sometimes we have a credible baseline, and we have actions we can describe, but we never stop to measure the impacts of our actions. Those stories have a beginning and middle, but no end. For example, 'We had 30 arrests in our community last year that an independent study showed were the result of racial profiling. We instituted new training for police officers.' That is not a story; it's a wind-up. What happened after the training? Did anything change? I think of these stories as cliffhangers because they never resolve.

The measurement process provides both the framework and the information for telling compelling stories. We can use these stories to attract resources to our work. Our stories leave a trail for others to follow and from which we and they can draw lessons and imagine new possibilities. The YGWYM process will allow you to effectively tell the story of your work.

The benefits of engaging in the measurement process include:

- clarifying what we are trying to achieve before we act;
- testing our assumptions so that we do not unnecessarily limit our sense of what is possible;
- helping us learn about the world around us through intentional reflection;
- developing information to create new feedback loops that change systems;
- supporting self-organizing behaviours and reducing the need for top-down bureaucratic control; and
- being able to tell compelling stories about our work.

Now that we know what measurement can allow us to do, we need to understand some basic measurement concepts and vocabulary.

Notes

1. The Town of Fairfield, Vermont (2019) 'Annual Report of the Town Year Ending December 31, 2019, Fairfield, Vermont' p. 5.
2. For a wonderful explanation of how changes in the structure of information flows (who does and does not have access to what kinds of information) can leverage systems change, see Meadows (1999).
3. Friends of Dragon Run, <https://www.dragonrun.org/paddle-season-information.html> [accessed 30 August 2022].

4. Ratner, S. (1997) *Emerging Issues in Learning Communities*, prepared for the Appalachian Regional Commission. This is one of three background readings we recommend for people who seek to become Measurement Guides.

References

Di Stefano, G., Gino, F., Pisano, G.P. and Staats, B.R. (2014, 2015, 2016) *Making Experience Count: The Role of Reflection in Individual Learning*, Harvard Business School Working Paper 14–093, Cambridge, MA.
Gladwell, M. (2000) *The Tipping Point: How Little Things Can Make a Big Difference*, Back Bay Books, Newport Beach, CA.
Himmelman, A.T. (2002) *Collaboration for a Change: Definitions, Decision-making Models, Roles, and Collaboration Process Guide*, Himmelman Consulting, Minneapolis, MN.
Koehrsen, W. (2018) 'Unintended consequences and Goodhart's law' [online], Towards Data Science. <https://towardsdatascience.com/unintended-consequences-and-goodharts-law-68d60a94705c> [accessed 6 January 2020].
Manheim, D. (2019) '240: Goodhart's Law and why metrics fail (David Manheim)', Rationally Speaking Podcast with Julia Galef [online], 16 September. <https://www.digitalpodcast.com/feeds/30862-rationally-speaking> [accessed 6 February 2023].
Meadows, D. (1999) *Leverage Points Places to Intervene in a System*, The Sustainability Institute, Hartford, VT. <https://bsahely.com/2018/08/07/leverage-points-places-to-intervene-in-a-system-by-donella-meadows/> [accessed 12 December 2020].
Nystrom, R.J., Duke, J.E.A. and Victor, B. (2013) 'Shifting the paradigm in Oregon from teen pregnancy prevention to youth sexual health', *Public Health Reports* 128(Suppl 1): 89–95. <https://doi.org/10.1177%2F00333549131282S110>.
Oregon Health Authority, Oregon Public Health Division (2015) *Oregon Youth Sexual Health Report: Five Year Update*. <https://www.oregon.gov/oha/ph/HealthyPeopleFamilies/Youth/YouthSexualHealth/Documents/YHSP5YrUpdate.pdf> [accessed 15 January 2021].
Ratner, S. (1997) *Emerging Issues in Learning Communities*, Yellow Wood Associates. <https://www.yellowwood.org/assets/resource_library/resource_docs/emergingissuesinlearningcommunities.pdf> [accessed 8 September 2020].
Rutledge, P. (2011) 'The psychological power of storytelling' [blog], *Psychology Today*, 11 January. <https://www.psychologytoday.com/us/blog/positively-media/201101/the-psychological-power-storytelling> [accessed 14 February 2020].
Schautz, J.W. and Conway, C.M. (2016) *The Self-help Handbook for Small Town Water and Wastewater Projects*, The Rensselaerville Institute, Delmar, NY.
Wheatley, M.J. (1994) *Leadership and the New Science*, Berrett-Koehler Publishers, San Francisco.

CHAPTER 3

Measurement vocabulary and an overview of the measurement process

You Get What You Measure uses a vocabulary that consists of words that are in common use – goal, indicator, assumption, action, and measure; however, the success of this process relies on very specific definitions of each word. Because *You Get What You Measure* uses these words in specific and often unfamiliar ways, we always ask people who are learning the process to take all the meanings and associations that they already have with each word, tie them up in a pretty box, wrap a ribbon around it, and put it in the back of their mind so that they can come to the definitions we use afresh. Please take a moment to do this before reading further. The definitions you already know will still be there if you choose to retrieve them later.

We also strongly advise you NOT to try to compare our definitions of these words with other words you may understand to be similar. So, for example, we suggest that your time will not be well spent trying to compare our meaning of the word 'goal' with the meanings you have learned for the word 'objective', or our meaning of the word 'indicator' with meanings you have learned for the word 'measure'. You are likely to confuse yourself *and* lose the opportunity to develop clarity that can come with shared understanding of the specific definitions we offer. Sometimes it is best not to try to build on what you already know; this is one of those times.

The next few paragraphs explain how we define each term and why we define it the way we do.

Goal

In the context of You Get What You Measure, a goal is a condition you wish to achieve. A goal is *not* an action. It is *not* about doing or making; it is about being. Achieving a goal requires a change in the way you, your organization, your community, or the world around you looks, feels, and acts.

It is quite common for organizations to define their 'goals' as activities. For example, one community we worked with had the 'goal' of creating jobs. Creating jobs is an activity, it is something you do; being a community in which everyone who wants a job has one is a condition. When goals are defined as conditions, we can begin to recognize that there are many different things that need to change to make progress toward the condition we seek. Conversely, when we define our 'goals' as actions, we fixate on the actions and all too often lose sight of why we are doing them in the first place.

Often, we have an implicit goal or a condition that we are trying to achieve that has never been stated out loud (the examples of Everyday Measurement in Chapter Two illustrate implicit goals). The best way to uncover an implicit goal is to ask, 'Why?' Why are we doing the things we have chosen as our primary activities? What is the condition we are trying to create? In a community that has focused all their efforts on creating jobs, one might ask, 'Why are we creating jobs?' One answer might be, 'So that we can attract more young people to our community.' The next question would be, 'Why do we want to attract more young people to our community?' The answer might be, 'So that we have enough of a tax base to support our school and town services.' Okay, so the condition we want to achieve is to be a town that has enough tax revenue to support its school and town services. Is creating jobs the only way to get there? Probably not. Is it the best way? Maybe, but maybe not.

Until clarity is achieved about the condition you are trying to create, it is difficult to recognize all the possible contributors to that condition that need to be addressed to make progress. It is all too easy (and common) to latch onto a single action as a 'silver bullet' that is likely to ultimately disappoint. Pushing even further may reveal even more about underlying conditions. For example, if asked why the community is so concerned about having enough taxes to support local services, the answer might be, 'Because we are afraid of losing our school.' Why? 'Because our school is the centre of our community and without it we will lose our sense of ourselves.' If this is the issue, then the desired condition or goal could be stated as, 'We are a community with a strong sense of ourselves.' Sometimes it takes a cascade of 'whys' to get to a condition. For more on getting to goals, please see Chapter Four.

Here is another example. A client came to us with the 'goal' of creating a community centre. This is an activity, not a condition. The first time we asked them 'Why?' they said, 'To make better use of a vacant building in the town centre.' The second time we asked 'Why?' they said, 'To make more activities available in our community for people of all ages.' The third time we asked 'Why?' they said, 'So that older people and younger people in our community have positive interactions on a regular basis.' Now *that* is a condition. Once stated, it becomes possible to recognize that there are many ways to create that condition that may or may not include creating a physical community centre.

If we organize around a single action (or suite of related actions), we fail to see the larger system that shapes the condition we have now and the implicit goal which is the condition we seek. We often size our choice of actions (that become our 'goals') to fit what we assume are the capacities and capabilities of our organization. It is a short but often crippling step from there to assuming that, based on the actions that are under our control as an individual or a single organization, we can make a real difference at scale on our own. If we are working on social change, the challenges are generally multi-faceted, and often a single group cannot address every contributing factor by themselves, nor do they have the clout to enact the systems changes needed to see progress at scale. *Defining 'goals' as actions is a common worst practice that helps individual organizations justify their existence and keeps our collective heads in the sand regarding the full scope of changes required.*

The answer to the question 'why' will be different based on place, context and involved stakeholders, even when the groups are focused on the same action. In another place that has focused their activities on creating jobs, for example, when asked 'why?' the answer was, 'Because too many people in our community are unemployed, and we want everyone in our community who wants a job to be able to have one.' The condition we want to achieve is, 'We are a community where everyone who wants a job has one.' To make progress toward this condition or goal, there are likely to be many things that must be addressed; creating jobs by itself will not suffice. For example, we may need to address barriers like transportation, education, training, health conditions, childcare, language barriers, racism, sexism, ageism, hiring practices, communication skills, and even lack of appropriate wardrobes.

A lack of job opportunities may not even be the most important barrier to address to make progress toward the goal. For example, in south central New York, the problem is not the availability of jobs, it's the location of the jobs in relation to the labour force. There are well over 1,000 unfilled jobs in the area but many of the jobs are outside the most populated areas and are difficult for potential job seekers to access.[1] In this instance, the action taken has been to develop a multi-purpose wealth creation transportation value chain that connects potential workers to employers while building stocks of multiple forms of wealth in the community.[2]

The first step in making progress toward a desired goal or condition is to make our understanding of that goal explicit. After that, we can better understand the full range of stakeholders who will need to be engaged to make progress. If our goal is ambitious, the efforts of many individuals and organizations with different self-interests will need to be aligned. Before diverse organizations can work effectively together to make progress toward the goal, they need to be able to share their perceptions of what the goal means to them and to their constituents. This is where indicators come in.

Indicator

Goals stated as conditions as in 'Everyone in our community who wants a job has a job,' or 'At least half of our residents age 25+ have a baccalaureate degree,' or 'The economy of our region is strengthened by the arts,' may seem straightforward at first glance but in reality they mean something different to each person and/or organization who sees them. Whereas many strategic planning processes assume the goal means the same thing to everyone who sees it, we know this is rarely, if ever, the case. The *You Get What You Measure* process uses indicators to unpack the meaning of goals, reveal values, and create the foundation for systems analysis.

We define an indicator as something that must be changed, or a condition that must be achieved, in order to claim that progress is being made toward a goal. Sometimes we need more of something, sometimes less. Sometimes we need to create something that does not exist now and sometimes we need to get rid of existing barriers. An indicator is *not* a measure. A good indicator is relatively specific and clearly related to the goal. It answers the questions, 'What are the most important things that need to change in current reality, and in which direction, for you and your constituents to be convinced that progress is being made toward the goal?' Since there are many ways to interpret goals depending upon one's life experiences, values, and priorities, there are also many possible indicators that could suggest progress toward the goal.

A discussion of indicators is a discussion of values and priorities – it reveals how different people interpret the goal and what aspects of the goal matter most to them. Indicators are most powerful when created and agreed upon within the context of the community, region, or organization where they have real meaning to participants. Therefore, *You Get What You Measure* does not rely on predetermined lists of indicators. For more on indicators, please see Chapter Five. A key leverage indicator emerges from the indicator analysis as a powerful starting point for changing an entire system. Key leverage indicators will be explained in detail in Chapter Six.

Assumption

An assumption is a hypothesis about some aspect of the way the world works that we believe to be true. We all make assumptions all the time because we cannot know everything that we need to know to make good decisions. The problem is that often our assumptions are incorrect. False assumptions limit our sense of what is possible. For example, it was once assumed that an electrical signal could not travel more than 100 metres. If Marconi and others had not challenged that assumption, we would not have wireless communications, among many other things.

Assumptions can be difficult to recognize because they are often deeply embedded in the way we think about the world. There are also assumptions embedded in how we think about the most important things that need to change in current reality to make progress toward the goal. There are assumptions embedded in how we think one indicator relates to another. Challenging, and sometimes even identifying our assumptions can make us very uncomfortable, fearful, and defensive, but the tendency to treat our assumptions as unquestionably true allows them to shape our world and become barriers to innovation and creativity. *You Get What You Measure* helps create a safe space to generate the curiosity to surface assumptions that may be limiting and find ways to test them. Assumptions will be further explained in Chapter Six.

Measure

A measure provides a way to count or value the status of an indicator. For example, things may be measured in terms of 'number of', 'percentage of', 'quality of', 'frequency of', or 'rating of', to name a few. To track a measure over time, you must have a **unit** which defines what you are counting (metres, people, litres, hours, etc.) and a **baseline** which defines the value of the measure at some predetermined starting point. There are many ways to measure, including, but not necessarily limited to, using physical instrumentation, direct measures, indirect or unobtrusive measures, and participant observation. We derive measures by carefully defining our indicators in behavioural terms. Measures, including baselines, framing measures, and measurement plans, will be explained in detail in Chapters Seven, Eight, and Nine.

Action

An action (or intervention) is something you do in order to achieve your goal. Actions are designed to move measures of key indicators toward our goals. We use the results of measurement to assess the effectiveness of our actions. Actions matter only in so far as they are helping us make progress toward our goals. Actions are not the starting point of our process, but are the last things to consider and to bring into play, since we must understand our goals, key leverage indicators, and measures before we can design useful actions. Actions will be further explained in Chapter Ten.

Figure 3.1 is the handout we use with stakeholders to introduce them to the You Get What You Measure vocabulary.

Now that we have defined the basic terms, let's look at an overview of the entire measurement process as illustrated in Figure 3.2.

An overview of the measurement process

You Get What You Measure begins with identifying goals (please see Chapter Four for more on how we do this). Goals are the conditions we wish to achieve through our work. Goals should reflect what we really want, not what others tell us we should want. Goals that resonate with stakeholders are the foundation for meaningful measures. The way we express our goals may change over the course of the measurement process as we become clearer and better educated about what is really going on around us and what is possible.

The process moves from identifying goals to discovering indicators, or the things that need to change in current reality to be able to say that progress is being made toward each goal. There are no wrong indicators; indicators are expressions of the life experiences, values, and priorities of stakeholders.

You Get What You Measure

Measurement Vocabulary

Goal

A goal is a condition that you wish to achieve. A goal is not an action. It is not about doing or making; it is about **being**. Achieving a goal requires a change in the way your organization or your community looks, feels, and acts. For example, creating jobs is an activity; being a community in which everyone who wants a job has one is a goal. Goals are usually broadly stated. A well-chosen goal should reflect what you really want, not what you think someone else, like a funder, wants to hear.

Indicator

An indicator is something that must be changed, or a condition that must be achieved, in order to claim that progress is being made toward a goal. Since goals are generally quite broad, there are many possible indicators that could suggest progress toward the goal.

A discussion of indicators is a discussion of values – it reveals how different people interpret the goal. Indicators are most powerful when created and agreed upon within the context of the community or organization where they have real meaning to participants.

Action

An action (or intervention) is something you **do** in order to achieve your goal. The action should be defined broadly enough to involve people in a variety of different tasks and provide opportunities for participants who don't normally work together to do so.

Successful actions build energy and produce spin-offs. They broaden our perspective and suggest new relationships and possibilities.

Assumption

An assumption is a hypothesis about some aspect of the way the world works that we believe to be true. Assumptions can be difficult to recognize because they are often deeply imbedded in the way we think about the world. The tendency to treat our assumptions as unquestionably true allows them to shape our world and become barriers to innovation and creativity. False assumptions limit our sense of what is possible. For example, it was once assumed that an electrical signal could not travel more than 100 metres. If Marconi and others had not challenged that assumption, we wouldn't have wireless communications, among many other things.

Measure

A measure provides a way to actually count or value the status of an indicator. For example, things may be measured in terms of 'number of', 'percentage of', 'quality of', 'frequency of', or 'rating of'. To track a measure over time, you must have a <u>unit</u> which defines what you are counting (metres, people, litres, hours, etc.) and a <u>baseline</u> which defines the value of the measure at some predetermined starting point.

Figure 3.1 Measurement vocabulary handout
Source: © Yellow Wood Associates, Inc.

Once indicators have been identified and clarified they are analysed in a systems context in which key leverage indicators and key results indicators emerge. Key leverage indicators drive the entire system of interrelated indicators toward the goal and key results indicators are

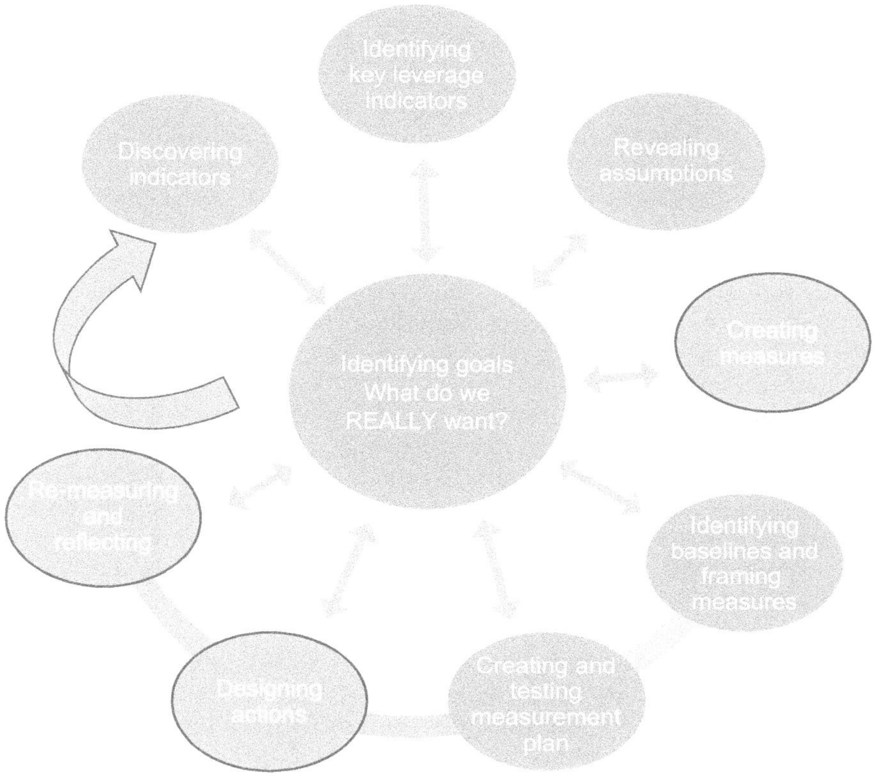

Figure 3.2 Overview of the measurement process

most likely to materialize as progress happens. For example, a group of diverse social change practitioners in the Virgin Islands defined a goal as 'Our island's people embrace moral living/virtues.' From an analysis of indicators in relation to the goal, there were three key leverage indicators driving change toward the goal in the entire system, listed in order of their influence:

1. A healthier and more sustainable physical and social environment.
2. More conveying of cultural values through stories, experiences, and habit-forming activities that encourage moral behaviour.
3. An increase in life skills classes for youth.

The key results indicators, or the changes that would be expected to occur over time based on positive changes in the key leverage indicators, were:

1. Fewer people tolerate/accept oversexualization in our island's cultural expressions.
2. Our community experiences fewer reported crimes as we embrace moral living.

Analysing indicators reveals the key assumptions that are being made about the relationships between indicators and between indicators and goals. If our assumptions are incorrect, the validity of the analysis will be affected. Therefore, it is important to identify and find ways to test our key assumptions. The process for deriving key leverage and key results indicators is described in greater detail in Chapters Five and Six.

Once we have defined goals, identified indicators, and performed an indicator analysis to find the key leverage and results indicators, the next step involves developing measures for these indicators. We know the condition we are trying to achieve; we know the most powerful behaviours that must change to drive the entire system toward that condition; now the question is, how will we recognize the change if it happens? Chapter Seven covers how measures are created.

After measures are created and tested, we identify baseline conditions (the beginning of our story) and we develop framing measures to create context and understand the amplitude of the impact we need to have in order to make a recognizable and significant difference. Framing measures help us create realistic targets around which we will design our activities or interventions, a process that will be described in Chapter Eight. Interventions or actions are designed to move measures of key leverage indicators toward the goals so that the entire system changes in a positive direction.

When we have enacted interventions or actions and given them enough time to make a difference, we measure the impacts and reflect on them and begin the process of refinement as described in Chapter Ten. We may find ourselves refining goals, indicators, and measures as well as interventions as we learn more about current reality. The measurement process is an iterative process that leaves space for learning as we go and refining our assumptions accordingly. Instead of tying us to a fixed set of activities, it releases our creative juices to find the best ways to achieve our goals considering what we learn as we progress and as the world changes around us.

Communication skills

Before we begin the measurement process in earnest, we start by practising skilled inquiry and skilled listening,[3] two skills critical to creating a safe environment for diverse stakeholders that Measurement Guides should be able to model for participants. Depending on the dynamics of the group and the time available, Measurement Guides may choose to invite all participants to engage in a short training related to skilled inquiry and skilled listening.

Skilled inquiry

The purpose of skilled inquiry is to ask questions which assist an individual or group in discovering their own wisdom and insights. This skill differs from the usual expert mode of giving advice or solving problems for others.

There are two ground rules for skilled inquiry:

- Ask questions that come from a place of not knowing the answers. You must be genuinely curious. This means approaching people and situations with the openness of a learner, and relinquishing the mindset of 'expert'.
- Ask questions that only the person or people you are asking could answer. You must ask questions that draw out the personal experiences, perceptions, and interpretations of those you are questioning. For example, a question such as 'What is it like for you to be an Extension professional?' is a legitimate example of skilled inquiry, while 'Do you know how to lead a group?' is not. The latter could be determined through observation or conversation with others, the former could not.

Skilled inquiry is most powerful when the inquirer maintains a non-judgemental attitude and avoids the temptation to give advice. If the person or people you are inquiring of ask you what they should do, your job is to ask them what has worked for them in the past, or what they have done in similar situations, rather than supply them with your own answer.

Skilled listening

The purpose of skilled listening is to learn about the person to whom you are listening, as well as yourself. To put space and awareness between what you hear and how you react.

There are four steps to skilled listening:

1. *Monitor your inner reactions.* When you are listening, notice how you feel about what you are hearing. Does it make you feel secure, scared, angry, sad, happy?
2. *Analyse your own reaction.* Why are you feeling that way? What is the story you are telling yourself about what you are hearing?
3. *Describe your reaction to the other person.* When you said X, I felt Y. The story I tell myself when I hear that is …
4. *Use skilled inquiry* (see above) to understand the other person's point of view: 'I want to check this out with you. I am hearing X; is that what you are saying?'

Skilled listening is an antidote to over-personalizing our communications. Often, we overreact or react inappropriately to other people because we assume that their communication is about us or means something about us that is not at all what they intended. Skilled listening encourages us to check out our assumptions before we act on them. Skilled listening also helps us become aware of the stories we tell ourselves about the stories we hear from others. We all have conversations going on in our heads that we are often aware of only intermittently at best. Becoming more aware of what is going on in our own minds as we listen may be challenging at first, but over time

✎ Exercise 3.1 Skilled listening and skilled inquiry

We practise skilled inquiry and skilled listening in groups of three. One person shares a quandary in their life that they are trying to work through. One person practises skilled inquiry, drawing the speaker out about the quandary they present. The third person practises skilled listening by dividing a piece of paper into two columns. In the column on the left they make notes about what they are hearing from the person with the quandary and in the column on the right they make notes about what they are telling themselves about what they are hearing, including how they feel about what they are hearing. After about 10 minutes, the roles rotate, and a new person becomes the storyteller, the inquirer, and the listener. There is a second rotation so that each person has practice with each role, and then the entire group debriefs. Debrief questions typically include:

- 'When you were the storyteller, did this conversation feel different to you from the types of conversations you typically have? How?'
- 'When you were the inquirer, did you find yourself wanting to give advice? What happened when you couldn't?'
- 'When you were the listener, did you learn anything about the stories you tell yourself that surprised you?'
- 'Which role was the easiest for you and which was the more difficult? Why do you think that was?'

it helps us become less distracted by our own inner dialogue and more open to hearing the person who is speaking to us.

Now that you have an idea of the complete *You Get What You Measure* process, it is time to dig in, beginning with goals.

Notes

1. Personal communication with J. Salo, Executive Director, Rural Health Network of South Central New York, 2019.
2. For more information on wealth creation value chains and multiple stocks of wealth, see Ratner (2020).
3. Material on skilled listening and skilled inquiry has been adapted from a workshop with Judy Sorum Brown and is available in Brown (2008).

References

Brown, J.S. (2008) *A Leader's Guide to Reflective Practice*, Trafford Publishing, Bloomington, IN.

Ratner, S.E. (2020) *Wealth Creation: A New Framework for Rural Economic and Community Development*, Routledge, New York.

CHAPTER 4
Getting to goals

The first step in measurement work is to make implicit goals explicit. (See Chapter Three to understand what we mean by the word 'goal'.) We do this in two steps by going first from values to themes and then from themes to goals. These exercises can be used in a variety of contexts to explore values related to a place, whether a specific community or region or building, or to explore values related to a topic such as the health care system, energy sources and uses, the environment, teen pregnancy, or food systems. Any number of stakeholders can participate in this stage of the work. Please return to Chapter Two for more information on identifying stakeholders to participate in *You Get What You Measure*.

Values

The things that people value are the things that matter to them. These things can be experiences, thoughts, feelings, memories, physical objects, relationships, and so on. What people value reflects their life experience, who they are, and how they choose to live. Sometimes the things we value most, or that we invest the most in, are the very things we take for granted. It is not until we name them, or we hear someone else name them that we fully appreciate how much they matter. Shared experiences like a natural disaster or a pandemic can cause us to reassess what we value individually and collectively.

When we ask people 'What do you value about your community (or another topic)?' we are using value as a verb, not as a noun. We are not asking, 'What are your values?' to which one might answer 'honesty, integrity, curiosity' or other abstractions, but rather 'What do you value about X?' We are attempting to elicit lived experiences, not abstractions. In making a list of what we value about something, whether it is a place, a situation, or an experience, we are making a list of what matters to us in relation to it. What we value can be aspirational; in other words, we can express what we would value in a system that works the way we would want it to, and/or we can express what we value about the way things are.

Themes

Within the context of You Get What You Measure, a **theme** is a thread that runs through a collection of individual responses about what is valued. A theme identifies the common elements of different individual responses.

For example, if we asked a group of stakeholders in a rural community in the rural north-eastern United States, 'What do you value about your community?' we might get the following responses:

Always seeing people I know

The view of the mountains from Lake Road

The people in my hiking group

Clean water I can drink from the tap

Friendly neighbours

Places to cross-country ski without paying a fee

Being able to swim in the lake

There would be many possible ways of arranging these into themes. One theme might be *the people who live here*. The values under that theme would include always seeing people I know and friendly neighbours. Another theme might be *recreational opportunities*. The values under that theme would include places to cross-country ski without paying a fee and being able to swim in the lake. A third theme might be *environmental quality* that could include clean water I can drink from the tap and the view of the mountains from Lake Road. Often the same response will fit into more than one theme. For example, 'the people in my hiking group' could fit into both the people who live here and recreational opportunities.

The things that show up on the list of values may vary considerably based on the focus of the work and on where and with whom you are working. Regardless of the variations, the purpose of identifying themes is to discover what it is that participants value in common.

Goals

Within the context of You Get What You Measure, goals are always stated in the *present tense*.

Instead of 'Our community will develop and maintain a variety of accessible recreational options for people of all ages and abilities,' which is an *activity*; a goal statement would be, 'Our community has a variety of accessible recreational options for people of all ages and abilities,' which is a condition.

This is more than mere semantics. When we state a goal in the future tense, it loses its power. When will we have it? It is aspirational but not compelling. When we state a goal in the present tense, we are confronted with a powerful psychological dissonance between what we know to be true today (limited recreational options) and what we aspire to. As long as we hold on to the goal and don't give up on it, that psychological dissonance will propel us in the direction of the goal. Think of it as a rubber band. If reality is one end of the band, but we state our aspiration in the current tense, we have stretched the rubber band. As long as we don't let go of the goal and

🖉 Exercise 4.1 Values to themes

Objectives: To share what we value individually
             To practise listening and asking clarifying questions
             To recognize the commonalities among our individual values

Materials: Pencil/pen for each participant, reflection worksheet,
            3 × 5 index cards, 5 × 8 index cards, rubber bands

Time: 30 minutes

Procedure:

1. Review the definition of **value** and discuss the instructions for identifying what matters to us as individuals.
2. Take three minutes for each participant to reflect on what they value in relation to the issue at hand. It could be what they value about the community, the economy, the health care system, the education system, and so on.
3. Share what participants value around the room or in breakout rooms with each participant contributing one thing that they value per round until all have been shared. Others ask clarifying questions and each participant or a facilitator or recorder writes each clarified value on a separate note card using the words of the participant. Be sure the writing is legible.
4. Place all cards face up on a table.
5. Review the definition of **theme**.
6. Have all participants assemble around the table and silently sort the cards into themes. Before they begin, explain that if a card keeps getting moved between two themes, they should simply make a duplicate card so that it appears in both places. When participants have stopped moving cards back and forth, there should be some number of card clusters on the table.
7. Hand a cluster of cards to a subset of participants and ask them to talk with each other to come up with a word or a short phrase that captures the thread running through all the values in the cluster. That is the **theme**. Once they have a theme, they should write it down on a larger card and bundle the values with it.
8. Have each group read the cluster of values they were given and then share the theme with the larger group. Discuss and modify the theme if needed.

let the rubber band go slack, the tension in the rubber band will help pull us toward the goal. If we give up on the goal and let the band become slack, we will backslide toward current reality. If we define the goal in the future tense, we do not create any tension at all. There is no dissonance between what we have now and what we 'will have' in the future.

Stating a goal in the present tense is not lying. We all understand the goal to be aspirational. Stating the goal in the present tense encourages us to imagine it in its fullness and creates an energy that can help propel us in the right direction. We can take advantage of the power of dissonance. Martin Luther King called our attention to the power of dissonance in his Letter from Birmingham City Jail. He called it 'creative tension', and said,

> There is a type of constructive, nonviolent tension which is necessary for growth. Just as Socrates felt it was necessary to create a tension in the mind so that individuals could rise from the bondage of myths and half-truths to the unfettered realm of creative analysis and objective appraisal, we must see the need of having nonviolent gadflies to create the kind of tension in society that will help men to rise from the dark depths of prejudice and racism to the majestic heights of understanding and brotherhood ... We are not the creators of tension. We merely bring to the surface the hidden tension that is already alive. We bring it out in the open where it can be seen and dealt with (King, 1963: 2).

Stating goals in the present tense brings the dissonance between desired conditions and actual conditions to the surface.

The process we use to make implicit goals explicit is inclusive and allows participants to begin to practise skilled listening and skilled inquiry early. By asking participants to identify what matters to them, we avoid the tendency of watching a group define their goals not in terms of what matters most to them, but rather in terms of what they think someone else in authority or a funder or boss wants to hear. In our experience, when a group does the work of articulating goals that reflect what matters most to them, they are a solid step closer to engaging the resources required to make progress toward those goals and far less likely to self-sabotage down the road.

The Community Foundation of South Wood County, Wisconsin convened a wide range of local and regional non-profit organizations to develop shared goals. Figure 4.1 shows several of the values, themes, and goals that emerged. Notice the range of different ways that participants expressed what they value. Also notice how goals were crafted around a common theme, taking into consideration the content of the values.

External and internal goals

There are two broad types of goals that should be articulated. We call the first type *external goals*. External goals refer to the conditions that a group of stakeholders want to bring about in the world. The second type are *internal goals*. Internal goals refer to the conditions that need to be present within the stakeholders' own organizations to make progress toward the external goals. You Get What You Measure typically focuses first on articulating external goals and then considers internal goals in light of them.

✎ Exercise 4.2 Themes to goals

Objectives: To craft themes into statements of condition or goals using the
proper form for a goal statement
To practise listening and asking clarifying questions

Materials: Pencil/pen for each participant, stack of value cards with theme
card on top, flip chart paper and marker

Time: 30 minutes

Procedure:

1. This activity builds on Exercise 4.1: Values to themes (see above). Hand each
   small group of people a single stack of values with the theme on top. The
   size of the small working group will depend on the size of your gathering.
   A good size for these working groups is three to six people. We recommend
   one Measurement Guide for every 30 participants. A group of 30 is likely
   to think of several themes and there may be four to six small groups tasked
   with coming up with goals.
2. Review the definition of **goal** as a condition and not an activity.
3. Explain the importance of stating goals in the **present tense**.
4. Ask each small group to craft a goal that expands on the theme and
   reflects the values they were handed.
5. Have each group share their goal with the entire group. Discuss, reframe,
   and modify as needed. Be sure the goal is a condition stated in the
   present tense.

For example, an external goal for a food hub in Michigan was, 'There is
a profitable, resilient and socially just food system in Michigan.' The group
identified two internal goals that had to be achieved to enable their organization to contribute to progress toward the external goal. These were:
1) 'Our food hub is financially solvent while providing liveable wages
and benefits to its employees,' and 'Our food hub is an active community
partner and leader as well as being considered a valuable resource for
information on food.'

Prioritizing goals

Once a set of external and internal goals has been articulated, it can often be
very useful to prioritize them. This is important because trying to work on
too many goals at the same time defeats the power of the process to provide
focus and clarity. One goal is plenty; two is a lot; and three is probably too
many. More than three is delusional in most situations and is likely to lead to
frustration, lack of focus, and confusion. Very few organizations can effectively
pursue three things at the same time.

Values

- The ability to come together and create lasting change, providing a better life for those in our communities
- I value a community where advocates work collaboratively to achieve large goals
- The opportunity to pull agencies together to work as a team
- Our community as a whole – connectedness in this together (a broader circle of friends and family)
- Value people working together toward community goals
- Response to need with action and optimism
- Provide more opportunities for people from diverse groups to come and work together
- Seamless transition and communication between community services (education, non-profit, org.)
- In community today: connectedness and ability to mobilize networks (humane society, Agency of Human Services (AHS), etc.)
- Common networks of people throughout (familiar faces)
- Transportation
- People connected to community

Theme
Collaboration – A

Goal
People in our community are engaged and work across boundaries to make it a better place.

Values

- Pre-K thru post-secondary education opportunities
- Education – infants through technical college for young people
- Quality early-care and education
- Great library
- I value students receiving education that prepares them to live and work in a world economy
- Education
- I value education options in our community
- The synergy that area schools have created towards financial literacy of students in grades K-12
- Education opportunities (through the Community Foundation of South Wood County) for continuing to grow
- Quality schools/education (public and private)
- Available education opportunities
- I value a community that supports and embraces educational choices public and/or private
- Entrepreneurial innovative spirit
- Cultural life, the arts
- Value the people who provide high-quality childcare and education for all children
- Diverse education opportunities
- A community that values education – pre-K to adult

Theme
Learning/Education – B

Goal
We are a community that fosters high-quality, life-long education.

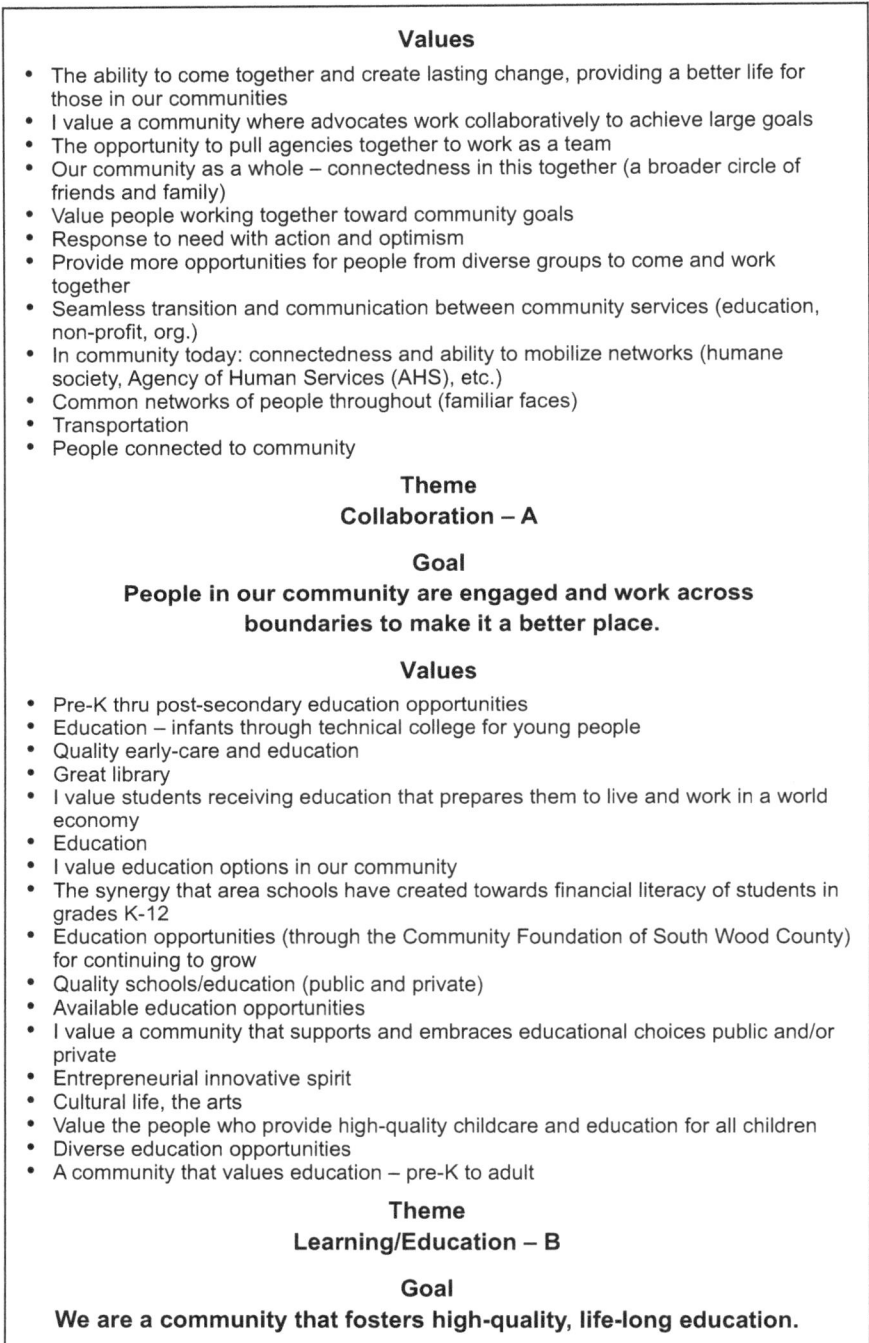

Figure 4.1 Sample values to themes to goals, South Wood, 2009

There are at least two ways to go about prioritizing goals. The first is to simply take the temperature of the group of stakeholders and determine which one or two goals the group has the most energy around. The second approach, which can be combined with the first, is to consider whether one goal would need to be achieved in whole or in part before another could be achieved. If the answer is 'yes', it makes sense to focus on the goal or condition that needs to be met first. When the YGWYM process is being used with a discrete organization or a defined partnership, it often makes sense to prioritize one external and one internal goal. Otherwise, keep the focus on a small number of external goals to start.

Understanding what each goal means

Now that you have a small set of priority goals (ideally, no more than three) derived from the values of your stakeholders, the next step in the measurement process is understanding what each stakeholder thinks matters most about each goal. This is a process that breathes. Each inhale gathers in information from stakeholders and each exhale results in greater understanding and specificity. Values to themes is an inhale and an exhale, as is themes to goals. Now the group is about to take another breath.

Unlike many processes, *You Get What You Measure* does not assume that the goal matters in the same way to everyone; in fact, we assume it matters in a different way to each person in the room. By taking the time at the beginning to figure out the range of what matters to stakeholders about each goal, we give every stakeholder a voice in the process and inoculate against the kind of passive aggressive behaviour that too often results when stakeholders feel they have not been heard or understood. Identifying what matters most about the goal from the perspective of each stakeholder lays the groundwork for a deeper understanding of the larger system that affects progress toward the goal. This is where indicators come in.

Reference

King, Jr, M.L. (1963) *Letter from a Birmingham jail*. <www.gracepresbytery.org/wp-content/uploads/2020/06/Letter-from-a-Birmingham-Jail-King.pdf> [accessed 31 August 2020].

CHAPTER 5
Indicators of progress

The power of visualization in social change work

Visualization refers to using one's imagination to form a mental image of something in as many dimensions – visual, kinesthetic, auditory, etc. – as possible. It is a powerful tool that can help stakeholders develop indicators of progress based on how they visualize the condition that represents the goal to which they are committed.

Experiments have been conducted that compare the performance of athletes who practise their sport in real time, athletes who both practise and visualize themselves performing, and athletes who only visualize themselves performing. Who do you think plays best? Answer: The athletes who both practise in real time and visualize themselves playing have been shown to outperform the others.

Visualization is not the same as vision or visioning. Community visions are verbal statements of a preferred future developed by a group of people. Visioning sessions result in vision statements. Often these vision statements are stated in the future tense. *You Get What You Measure* does not use vision statements. As previously discussed, YGWYM uses goals, which are distinguished from vision statements in that they are stated in the **present** tense.

Visualization is a process of using our full selves, not just our intellects, to discover what needs to change to show convincing progress toward our goals. Individuals visualize, not groups. Visualization answers the questions: What would it look like, feel like, sound like, smell like, taste like, seem like to be living in the desired condition today? What would need to change in current conditions to get closer to the goal? What changes in your behaviour, the behaviour of others, and other tangible things would be necessary and desirable?

We think one way to help people discover powerful indicators of change is by using guided visualization. When participants are given the opportunity to experience the desired condition or goal through visualization it often becomes more concrete and real to them. Then, when they compare that visualization of a desired condition with their experience of current reality, the behaviours and other tangible things that need to change to make progress toward the goal tend to stand out more clearly.

🖉 Exercise 5.1 Guided visualization

Objective: Create multi-sensory mental images of a condition or goal and compare it with current reality to identify the most important things that need to change to make progress.

Materials: Imagination and guiding questions

Time: 25 minutes

Procedure:

1. Select one goal at a time for this exercise.
2. Instruct participants to close their eyes if they wish and use their imaginations to create the condition they wish to see (this can be done for external and internal goals). How do you encounter that condition? What do you see? What do you touch? What do you taste? What do you smell? What do you hear? How does it make you feel? How do you behave? How do others behave? Allow at least a minute between each question. Invite participants to take notes if they wish.
3. Now visualize your encounter with current reality as it relates to this goal. What is the condition actually like for you right now? What do you see? What do you touch? What do you taste? What do you smell? What do you hear? How does it make you feel? How do you behave? How do others behave? Allow at least a minute between each question. Invite participants to take notes if they wish.
4. Place the current reality and your visualization of the goal side by side in your imagination. What are the differences? Based on your visualizations, can you name one or two of the most important things that would need to change in current reality for you to be confident that progress was being made toward the goal? Make a note of your observations and use your note to inform the indicator(s) you develop.

The definition and form of an indicator

One of the things that differentiates YGWYM from many other measurement and strategic planning processes is the way in which we define indicators. An indicator is something that must change or a condition that must be met so that a specific stakeholder can feel and report to others (i.e. their constituency) that meaningful progress has been made toward the goal. **An indicator is NOT a measure**. In fact, when we ask participants to develop indicators, we specifically tell them NOT to worry about what they think can and cannot be measured. The development of indicators should not be constrained by concerns about measurement.

Indicators are developed by individual stakeholders. They are not developed through a process of 'group think'. *Each indicator represents the most important thing that must change, from the perspective of the person that wrote it, to show that real progress has been made toward the goal. In this way, indicators are a reflection of values; they show what matters most to the person who wrote them in relation to the goal. Developing indicators before measures is a way of acknowledging the truth: any goal means different things to different people.* This fundamental truth is rarely acknowledged in other processes and often leads to miscommunication and failure to follow through with implementation.

It should be no surprise that the goal – an intentionally broad statement of desired conditions – means different things to different people based on their own life experiences, priorities, and values. Rather than brush this reality under the rug, YGWYM uses it to create an opportunity for stakeholders to learn from one another and to discover how what matters to each of them relates to what matters to others. Together, they can define the system they need to change to make meaningful progress and together they are able to define what meaningful progress really looks like.

For example, let's assume the goal is 'We are a safe community.' For one participant, the most important thing that has to change to make progress toward this goal is a stoplight at one specific intersection where many accidents now occur. For another, the most important thing is a reduction in domestic violence, and for a third it is adding a bike lane along Main Street. As long as each indicator is a genuine reflection of the values and life experiences of its contributor, at this stage of the process **there are no wrong indicators and there are no 'bad' indicators**. Each indicator is accepted as a genuine reflection of what matters most to the person who offers it.

Indicators have a specific structure. They are expressed in one of five ways.

1. More of, as in 'more people who want jobs have them and keep them'.
2. Less of, as in 'there is less trash along the roadsides'.
3. Presence of something that does not currently exist, as in 'there is a grocery store in our community'.
4. Absence or removal of something that currently exists, as in 'the rat-infested abandoned buildings in our community are torn down or rehabilitated'.
5. Something that is precious stays the same, as in 'people in our community continue to welcome strangers'.

This structure for indicators ensures that each indicator names the desired direction of change.

Developing and clarifying indicators

Indicators are developed and then clarified through sharing them with other stakeholders. Indicators are developed by individuals, not by groups. Once all participants have written down one or two indicators based on their experience with visualization, the next step is to have everyone share their indicators with the group one at a time.

The objective of this exercise is to be sure that each person feels heard and understood and that the group has a shared understanding about what the indicator means *to the person who wrote it*. Each indicator is equally valid since it reflects the views, values, and life experiences of the person contributing it, and none are discarded. Participants do not need to agree with the indicator; they just need to understand what it means to the person who wrote it. If we do not take the time to reach this understanding, we will fail to tap into the richness of experiences and perceptions related to our goal. Taking time to understand individual perspectives helps the entire group of diverse stakeholders appreciate the extent of their collective diversity.

The first time a person is asked to develop an indicator of progress, they may write a single word or they may write an entire paragraph. It is the job of the facilitator or Measurement Guide to draw them out about what they mean and how they see the connection between their indicator and the goal. No one else participates in this conversation; everyone else's job is to listen and learn. Once the person whose indicator it is has clarity about what they mean, they can be encouraged to rewrite the indicator as a short phrase.

Occasionally two people will come up with the same, or nearly the same, indicator. In this case, the two indicators may be combined into one with the permission of the authors. However, it is very important to *avoid over-generalization* and to maintain the distinctions between indicators where they exist. Do not be in a rush to combine them; instead seek to understand any important underlying differences in emphasis. For example, suppose two people came up with these indicators for the goal 'We are a safe community':

'Less availability of street drugs.'
'Fewer drug dealers on the street.'

A discussion might ensue in which the two indicators would either a) be combined by mutual agreement of the two authors, or b) be further differentiated. A combined indicator might be to use the first, 'Less availability of street drugs', if discussion reveals that this is what the person who wrote the second indicator was trying to get to. Two more differentiated indicators might be, 'Less availability of street drugs from every source' and 'Fewer drug dealers coming in from outside our community.' These are related, but they are not the same thing and the distinction may become important in the systems analysis.

Typically, each participant generates one indicator in relation to each goal that has been prioritized by the group. If the group is fewer than 10 people, they might each generate two indicators per goal. If more than 30 people are involved in the session, the work of developing and clarifying indicators can be done in smaller groups of 10–15 people and then shared with the larger group to address duplications and derive a complete set of indicators for each goal. The more people who are engaged in the process, the more time must be allowed for it.

Connecting the indicator to the goal

A strong indicator conveys to the group how the person who wrote it sees it connected to the goal. It is the job of the Measurement Guide to be sure that this connection is clear, both to the person who wrote the goal and to all the other participants. Some of the questions we ask to draw people out about how they see their indicator connecting to the goal are:

> 'What do you think will happen if this indicator changes in the desired direction?'

> 'How do you see the connection between a positive change in this indicator and progress toward the goal?'

Sometimes these questions will lead the author of the indicator to conclude that the connection to the goal is not very strong and they need to come up with a different indicator. Sometimes this discussion will result in greater clarity about how the author sees the connection to the goal. For example, suppose the goal was, 'We are energy self-sufficient,' and one participant came up with 'An increase in kilowatt hours produced locally'? A short discussion might reveal the possibility that more kilowatt hours could be produced locally without contributing to energy self-sufficiency. What if, for example, those kilowatt hours were exported from the community? Once the author has had a chance to think about it, he or she might clarify their thinking and edit the indicator to say, for example, 'More of the kilowatt hours we use locally are produced locally.' This has a much more direct connection to the goal.

Here is another example. Suppose the goal was, 'We have dynamic local leadership,' and one of the indicators was 'More youth advisers to local government'. A short discussion might reveal that the connection between the indicator and the goal could be strengthened in several ways, depending on the intent of the author. For example, 'More youth advisers to local government who are taken seriously by the adults and whose suggestions are used,' might be one way to strengthen the connection. 'More youth advisers that go on to become local leaders' might be another.

Here are two more examples of goals and a list of related indicators from our work in the field. The language is that of the participants.

Goal: There is a profitable, resilient, and socially just food system in Michigan.

Indicators:

1. Beginning farmers are able to access appropriately located, affordable, and productive farmland.
2. Fewer homes and farms are being lost to foreclosure (more debt is forgiven).
3. There are more food processors in the state which creates more sales channels for growers to diversify into.
4. Farm and food businesses at every step in the value chain operate unsubsidized externally.

✏ Exercise 5.2 Developing and clarifying indicators

Objectives:

- To give all stakeholders a voice in defining the system in relation to the goal. The system is defined by the entire collection of indicators of progress toward the goal and the interrelationships between them.
- To clarify indicators of progress so that each indicator reflects what its author intended, and the author feels heard and understood.
- To develop a shared understanding among all stakeholders working toward the same goal of what each indicator means to the person who wrote it and how the author relates the indicator to the goal.
- To create a group culture that recognizes and values the diversity of experiences and perceptions among stakeholders.

Materials: Pencils/pens and paper; 3 × 5 sticky notes

Time: Depends on the number of stakeholders; generally, at least 30 minutes and up to 90 minutes. This exercise should not be rushed. It is essential to engage each stakeholder equally in expressing their views about the most important things that need to change in current reality to make them confident that progress is being made toward the goal.

Procedure:

1. The Measurement Guide reviews the definition of an indicator and explains that there are no bad or wrong indicators. You do not have to agree with anyone else's indicator, you just have to do your best to understand what it means to the person who wrote it.
2. Each person shares a single indicator before anyone shares a second indicator. This ensures that each participant has an equal chance to be heard and allows the group to spot overlap and possible duplications as part of the sharing.
3. The Measurement Guide draws on each stakeholder to express what the indicator means and how they relate it to the goal. The Measurement Guide works with the author to rewrite the indicator clearly and concisely and in the appropriate form for an indicator. With permission of the participant who wrote the indicator, remove any excess words and any language about how the condition ought to be achieved. For example, a teenage participant contributed the following indicator: More tourism so that young people will stay here because they have places to work and interesting people to meet. Upon consultation with the participant, the indicator was shortened to: More variety of opportunities for young people to live and work here.
4. Once the indicator is in its final form, the author writes the indicator on a 3 × 5 sticky note and places it in the centre of the table.

5. More and more 'diverse' suppliers to our food hub.
6. Transparency of cost along the value chain must be consistent and available to all those participating in the process.
7. More customer/buyer education: for example the perception that local is more expensive; how to prepare whole foods; importance of local food.
8. More transparency of production practices (chemicals, fertilizers, genetically modified organisms, organic, etc.).
9. Policy supports (doesn't hinder) the growth and sustainability of small farmers.
10. Greater efficiency in the delivery chain.
11. More capacity for growing season extension.
12. More access to local food where people shop and eat.
13. Farmers and producers have reliable access to wholesale markets that provide a fair return on investment for their work.
14. More volume and diversity of local food is sold state-wide.
15. On-farm incomes increase.

Goal: Vermont landowners are intentional about contributing to Vermont's forest/wood products and services economy.

Indicators:

1. More landowners are active in forest management.
2. More landowners are involved in Current Use (a property tax incentive available to owners of agricultural and forestry land in Vermont).
3. More value-added activity in the Vermont forest/wood products sector.
4. More stories in the media about landowners working with the Vermont forest/wood products sector.
5. More advertising to landowners including more demonstration sites for landowners to visit that show how harvesting is good for the forest and compatible with other landowner goals.
6. More advertising to landowners that emphasizes the contribution they can make to local businesses and communities through sustainable forest management.
7. More economic returns for landowners through better information about demand and prices and revenue sharing along the value chain.
8. More and better information for loggers and consulting foresters to use with landowners.
9. Loggers are more service oriented in helping landowners meet multiple goals (not just cutting trees).
10. A procedure for notification to cut exists so that raw materials can be more effectively aggregated and supply can respond to demand.
11. More engagement in certification programmes such as ATF (American Tree Farm) and FSC (Forest Stewardship Council).
12. A comprehensive list of forest landowners in Vermont exists and is kept up to date.

Indicators should be as concise and precise as possible while conveying the full intent of the author. In Chapter Six we will be learning the process of indicator analysis. The value of the indicator analysis rests on maintaining a consistent interpretation of each indicator throughout. Indicators that are too wordy and/or abstract leave too much room for reinterpretation in the middle of an indicator analysis. The Measurement Guide has an important role in helping participants craft indicators that reflect their thoughts clearly, and an equally important role in making sure that everyone's indicator is understood by the whole group to mean what its author intended before entering into the indicator analysis. By honouring the meaning that each participant brings to their indicator in relation to the goal, the group shields itself from 'group think' and allows its collective thinking to be enriched by a diversity of life experiences.

CHAPTER 6
Indicator analysis for ordinary people

The indicator analysis is at the heart of the YGWYM process. The indicator analysis allows ordinary folks to become systems thinkers. Systems are simply relationships, both formal and informal, recognized and unrecognized, among and between entities. Systems thinking happens when we begin to recognize those relationships. Everything is part of a system. Some systems are large, and some are small. Effective measures help us learn about the system at the scale most appropriate to the goal we are trying to achieve. Our challenge is learning to recognize systems and learning how to focus in on systems at a scale that is meaningful but not overwhelming. If everything is connected to everything, where do we begin? Where do we end? A properly executed indicator analysis allows us to discover and eventually define the boundaries of the system most germane to our work and what drives it, based on the limits of our own current understanding of how the world works. It also allows us to surface our key assumptions about how the world works so that we can interrogate them and refine them as needed.

The process of engaging in an indicator analysis tends to break down artificial boundaries and 'turf' concerns among stakeholders as they grasp the relationships between what matters to them and what matters to others. Participants tend to become so absorbed in the analysis that they often forget which indicator was theirs to begin with. Even when they do not, since the laborious analysis process gives equal weight and consideration to each indicator, every voice is heard and valued. This tends to foster group cohesion and shared purpose.

Before beginning an indicator analysis, the group must have identified a goal or a series of goals (see Chapter Four) and discovered indicators for each goal (see Chapter Five). In addition, we have found it helpful to discuss the role of assumptions before beginning the indicator analysis. We often do this with an exercise called Everyday assumptions (see Exercise 6.1).

By beginning with the goal and asking participants to name the most important things that need to change in current reality for them to believe that real progress is being made toward the goal, we allow the elements of the system to be defined by its stakeholders. This is a powerful place to begin because it gives everyone a voice in establishing what is or is not part of the system based on their own lived experiences. The indicator analysis lets participants explore the relationships between their indicators and everyone else's indicators.

✎ Exercise 6.1 Everyday assumptions

Objectives:

- To increase awareness of the impact our assumptions have on our thinking and our behaviour.
- To acknowledge how scary it can be to recognize our assumptions as untested hypotheses about our world and its limitations.
- To create a safe space to consider what would be different if we found out our assumptions were incorrect.
- To become empowered to expand our sense of what is possible by identifying, reflecting on, and intentionally (re)creating our assumptions.
- To learn new methods to test our assumptions.

Materials: paper and writing implements

Time: approximately 15 minutes

Procedure:

1. Ask participants to write down one or two assumptions they have regarding some aspect of their life, whether career, family, their own abilities, or anything else. You might provide some examples, such as: I sent a colleague an email and they did not respond in a timely way. I assumed they didn't want to communicate with me so I felt hurt and I didn't want to reach out again. Several months later, I received a very friendly email back. My assumption was wrong; they were just overwhelmed. Here is another example: I worked with a client who assumed that the trajectory of a sector in their local economy was primarily determined by policies set outside it in another country. Research proved this assumption was incorrect. Many new opportunities for progress became evident as a result. We also hold many assumptions about other people as a group; we call these stereotypes. In general, this exercise works best when it is personalized and not directed toward broad societal issues.
2. Now ask participants to consider what would happen if they changed their assumption. How might it affect their thought process and/or behaviour? For example, if I assumed my colleague was overwhelmed, I might send a gentle reminder as a follow up instead of withdrawing from the relationship or spending energy harbouring bad feelings.
3. Next ask participants to consider one thing they might do to test their assumption. For example, sending a follow up email allows another chance for my colleague to let me know when they might be able to respond given their workload. Asking a third colleague to check in with the colleague I am trying to reach to determine why they haven't responded might be another option.
4. Give participants the opportunity to share their examples with one other person and/or with the whole group.

Worksheet

Everyday assumptions

1. Take a couple of minutes to write down one or two assumptions which may govern your behaviour in relation to something or someone that you care about.

2. Now think about what would happen if you were to change your assumption. How would your life be different?

3. Think of one thing you might do to test your assumption.

Figure 6.1 Everyday assumptions worksheet

   Upon completion, the analysis results in the identification of a small number of leverage points that will move the entire system toward the goal. Leverage points are the drivers of a system. They are the things that must change first before the entire system can realign toward the goal. Leverage points are starting places in producing powerful system-wide changes. We refer to these leverage points as **key leverage indicators**. Key leverage indicators form the basis for measures that are context specific and have meaning and value for a wide range of stakeholders in conveying progress, or lack thereof, toward shared goals. These measures are rooted in an overall systems analysis and everyone understands where they came from and why.

Analysing indicators in a systems context

The actual process of conducting an indicator analysis is very hands-on and uses simple materials – flip chart paper, sticky notes, and coloured markers. It is deliberately low tech and can be done anywhere at any time without the need for electricity, let alone an internet connection. Of course, it can also be readily adapted to a higher tech environment, but the power of the process comes from a group of stakeholders working together in real time. Here is how it works.

✎ Exercise 6.2 Analysing indicators in a systems context

Objectives:

- To engage stakeholders in discovering the interrelationships between indicators.
- To identify key assumptions regarding how the world works which, if incorrect, would materially affect the analysis.
- To identify areas of uncertainty where additional research is needed.

Materials: Flip chart paper, 3 × 5 sticky notes with one indicator written on each note, assortment of coloured markers – with as many different colours as there are indicators, pencils

Time: Required time will vary by the number of indicators, and the size and dynamic of the group. This exercise should not be rushed and can be expected to take a minimum of one hour per goal and as much as two or more hours.

Procedure:

1. Write the goal on the top of a piece of flip chart paper.
2. Write the indicators each stakeholder has identified and clarified, each on a separate sticky note or 3 × 5 card. This exercise works best when 10 to 16 indicators are used at one time although it can be done with many more indicators. The maximum number we have used is 35. That results in a very long process since the number of comparisons is double the number of indicators. In our experience, the number of key leverage indicators is between one and four regardless of the number of indicators used in the overall analysis. The Measurement Guide will want to work with participants to make sure that each indicator is distinct, none are exact duplicates, and to pare the number of indicators down if it seems excessive. One way to do this is to group similar indicators together and then rewrite a single indicator that captures the shared thinking. (See Chapter Five for more on developing and clarifying indicators.) It is important that all the indicators related to a single goal be included in one analysis.
3. Arrange the indicators in a circle on a large sheet of paper and number each indicator, beginning with number 1 in the 12 o'clock position. Explain to the group that the arrangement of indicators is completely arbitrary, and the numbers assigned to each indicator have no meaning; they are simply used for tracking purposes.

4. Read each indicator aloud and be sure everyone in the group understands what the indicator means to the person who wrote it. This is a short review of the process used to develop the indicators prior to the analysis. See Chapter Five for more details. It is important to honour and maintain the perspective and values represented by each indicator. Do not allow more powerful group members to overrule or alter an indicator because they disagree with it. Be sure everyone is clear about exactly what condition needs to change, and the desired direction of change.

5. Before they begin the analysis, ask the group if anyone thinks there is an essential indicator that is missing. If the group agrees, add it in. Decisions like these are generally arrived at through informal consensus.

6. Beginning with indicator 1, examine its relationship to each indicator around the circle. Ask yourself, 'If indicator 1 were to move in the desired direction, would it cause indicator 2 to change for the better (or, in its desired direction)?' **Consider this question in the short term** (based on current conditions and what the group believes about the way the world works – based in turn on any assumptions they may have coming into the analysis). (See Exercise 6.3 on Capturing assumptions). If the group agrees that the answer to this question is 'yes', draw a solid line between the two indicators with an arrow pointing to indicator 2. If some people in the group think there may be a causal relationship, but it is not very strong or clear, or if people in the group disagree, draw a dotted line between the indicators with an arrow. Disagreement indicates uncertainty or the lack of sufficient information to come to a convincing conclusion. Do not derail the analysis by trying to argue it out, simply note the disagreement and record it as a dotted line. If the group agrees that there is no connection between any two indicators, do not draw any line.

7. Resist the temptation to shorten the process by considering both directions of causation at the same time (for example 'Does A cause B? Or does B cause A?'). Keep the focus on one indicator at a time and whether a change in that indicator will cause a change in each other indicator around the circle. Go in order around the entire circle each time. Do NOT skip around.

   If, when you come to considering the two indicators a second time as you move around the circle (B in relation to A instead of A in relation to B), you find that the relationship is stronger in the opposite direction, simply cross out the original arrow and draw another. Sometimes it isn't obvious which way an arrow should go. In these instances, ask the group which direction they think is most likely under current conditions. Often thinking about it in concrete terms will bring clarity. If not, choose the direction in which the relationship is the strongest (i.e. if the arrow is dotted in one direction but solid in another, choose the solid arrow). Otherwise, choose the direction that the majority are most comfortable with. **Be sure that you do not have arrows going in both directions between any two indicators!**

8. When you are done, you will have a messy, colourful diagram, for example as illustrated in Figure 6.2

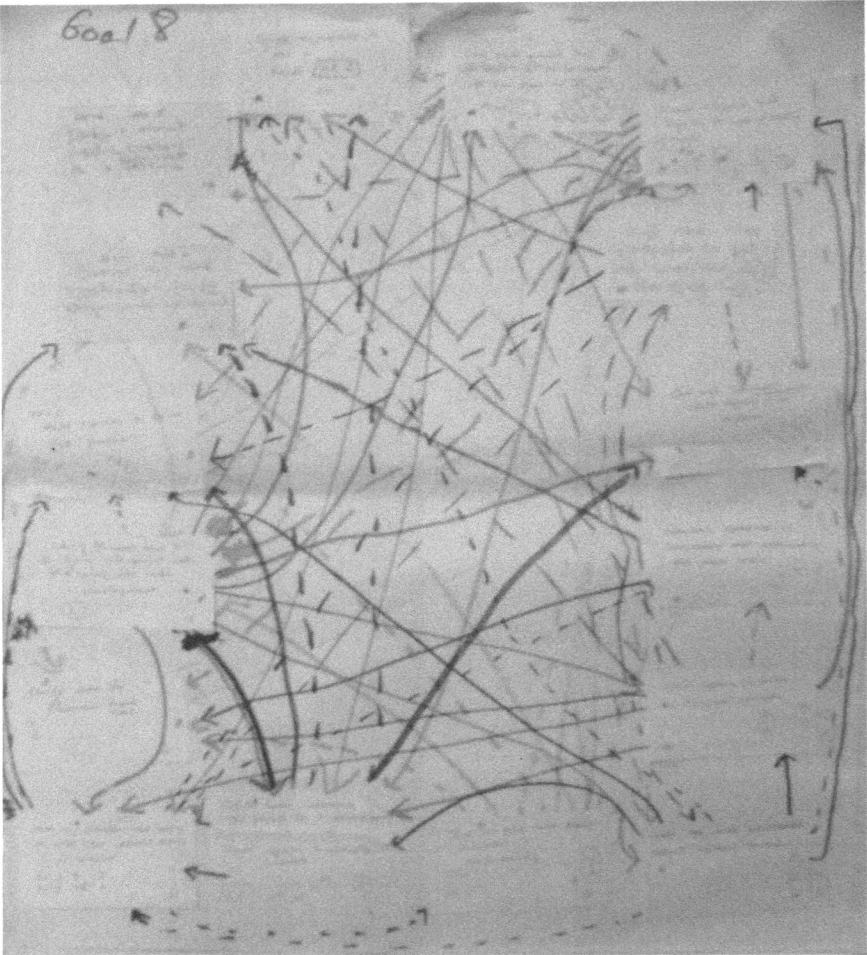

Figure 6.2 Indicator analysis

Hints on keeping participants engaged

The first part of the analysis can seem tedious to some participants. We find that a dose of chocolates in the centre of the table at about the halfway point (or whenever participants seem to be flagging) helps people get 'over the hump'. Stopping for a breath of fresh air or some calisthenics can also help people stay engaged as can changing roles for each indicator. Have one person read the indicators and state the question, 'If [indicator 1] changes in the desired direction, will it cause [indicator 2] to change in its desired direction?' The reader can also facilitate the discussion to see if the agreed answer is 'yes', 'no', 'maybe' or 'we disagree'. Have another person choose the coloured marker and draw the arrows for that indicator. Switch roles for the next indicator, and so on. As outlined in Exercise 6.3, the role of the person whose job it is to capture assumptions can also be rotated.

It is common for groups to come up with a shorthand for each indicator as the analysis progresses. Be sure that the initial meaning of the indicator is not lost along the way and that the interpretation of the indicator remains consistent throughout the analysis. Sometimes a group will agree to alter the meaning of an indicator. That is OK if the alteration is carried consistently through the analysis.

✎ Exercise 6.3 Capturing assumptions

'It isn't what we don't know that gives us trouble, it's what we know that ain't so'

Will Rogers

Objectives: To elevate awareness of key assumptions 'baked' into the analysis which, if they proved to be incorrect, would materially alter the results.

Materials: Paper and pen or pencil

Time: Will vary depending on the complexity of the analysis and the number of key leverage indicators. This exercise should be done while the indicator analysis is in progress and reviewed by the group after the indicator analysis is completed. Allow a minimum of 15 minutes to identify and record key assumptions.

Procedure:

1. Identify one or two stakeholders who will listen for assumptions as the indicator analysis proceeds. Assumptions are ideas about the way the world works that have not been tested or have not been tested in the context under consideration. Some assumptions may be implicit, some may be fully articulated, and others may be only partly articulated. Listeners may ask participants to explain their assumptions more fully as the analysis progresses.
2. Ask the listeners to record what they hear and sense about assumptions that are being made about each indicator as it is discussed in relation to every other indicator. Record assumptions as they relate one indicator to another. For example, if arrows were drawn between indicator #1 and indicators #2, 5, 7, and 12, the headings for recording relevant assumptions would be: #1 → #2; #1 → #5; #1 → #7 and #1 → #12. The listeners might want to record assumptions explaining why two indicators are not related as well. (Remember that the numbers that correspond with each indicator are completely arbitrary and only used for tracking purposes.)
3. Listeners continue to capture assumptions as each indicator is considered. The role of listener can be traded off during the analysis.
4. Keep your list of assumptions handy as they will be useful when you consider measurements and actions.

When you have completed the process of considering every indicator in relation to every other indicator and have captured the assumptions guiding the group's thinking about how indicators relate to one another, you are ready to 'score' the indicator analysis and discover the leverage points.

✏ Exercise 6.4 'Scoring' the indicator analysis

Objective: To identify key leverage and key results indicators. **Key leverage indicators** are the most powerful places to begin to move a system toward the goal. **Key results indicators** are the things most likely to change over time as a result of positive changes in the key leverage indicators.

Materials: The completed indicator analysis with sticky notes and coloured lines, pencils and coloured markers, list of assumptions by indicator

Time: Varies depending on the number of indicators. Generally, this exercise requires a minimum of 30 minutes.

Procedure:

1. On each sticky note that contains an indicator (or near it) create a grid as follows:

Solid out:	Solid in:
Dotted out:	Dotted in:
Total out:	Total in:

2. Count the number of solid and dotted outgoing arrows from each indicator and write the answers in the grid. Count the number of solid and dotted incoming arrows for each indicator and write those answers in the grid. Have at least two people do the counting to increase accuracy. The diagrams can be messy and it is easy to make mistakes, particularly if some arrows have been scratched out.
3. Add the total number of outgoing and incoming arrows for each indicator.
4. Identify the first, second, and third indicators with the most solid arrows going out and with the most total arrows going out. You might label them A, B, and C to distinguish them from the number of the indicator itself.
5. Beginning with the indicator with the most solid arrows going out, using the marker colour that was used to draw arrows from that indicator to others, place a coloured dot on all the indicators touched with an outgoing arrow (solid or dotted) by the indicator in question. If all the other indicators in the system have been touched, you have identified one key leverage indicator that will drive the entire system toward the goal.

If all the other indicators have not been touched, go through the same process with the indicator with the second highest number of outgoing arrows. Continue, if needed, with a third or fourth indicator. Though some indicators may be tied for the number of outgoing indicators, it is extremely rare that it takes more than four indicators, at the very most, to touch the entire system (see Figure 6.3).

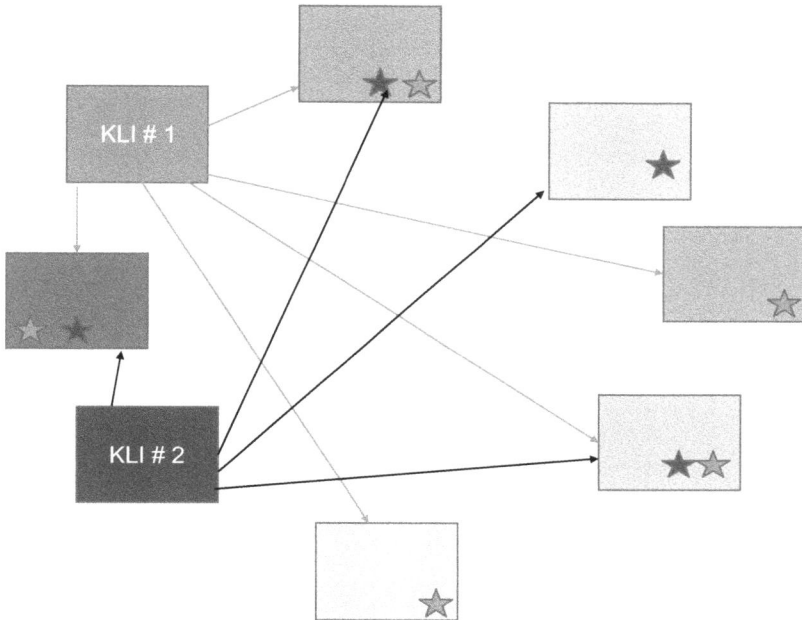

Figure 6.3 Mapping the impact of key leverage indicators (KLI) on the whole system

6. It is possible to end up with one or more 'orphan indicators'. These are indicators with no arrows either coming from them or coming into them from other indicators. 'Orphan indicators' are not integrated into the system as it is understood by the stakeholders. They may be part of another system related to a different goal.

7. Now consider the indicators with the most solid and dotted arrows coming into them from other indicators. Identify the one or two indicators with the most arrows coming in. There are generally one or two strong results indicators.

8. If you did not have a listener (or more than one) to identify assumptions during the above analysis stage itself, take the time now to identify the assumptions you made with respect to each indicator with the most arrows going out and its effect on each indicator it touches. Are there one or two assumptions which, if they are incorrect, would significantly change your diagram? What are they?

For example, in a community with a goal that 'In the year 2025, 40% of our residents age 25+ have a baccalaureate degree,' one of the key leverage indicators was, 'More third graders reading at grade level by the end of third grade.' As they discussed the impact of this indicator on all the other indicators in their analysis, they were able to identify the following three assumptions:

1. Expectation of college will impact student performance, desire.
2. Impacting youth will be easier/more effective than impacting adults.
3. Impacting families will impact all other indicators.

If any one of these assumptions were incorrect, it would affect the validity of their overall analysis. It will be important to return to these assumptions in developing measures, measurement plans, and actions.

Interpreting the indicator analysis

When the indicator analysis is complete, the group has a piece of flip chart paper covered in indicators connected by solid and dotted coloured arrows. Often, some arrows have been scratched out. The lines to which the arrows are attached may extend outside the circle of indicators. There does not seem to be a pattern at first glance. But there is! Interpreting the indicator analysis begins with counting arrows.

As discussed above, indicators with the most arrows leading out of them have the greatest leverage to change the whole system and push it toward the goal or desired new condition. Actions focused on these key leverage points are most likely to impact the entire system. The more solid arrows that are coming out of a key leverage indicator, the higher the degree of confidence that it will impact the other indicators positively over time. Therefore, if one key leverage indicator has five solid outs and three dotted outs and the next runner up has two solid outs and eight dotted outs, the indicator with the most solid outs would be the first key leverage indicator. Key leverage indicators are the places where powerful change can begin. They are upstream. Changes in key leverage indicators will ripple throughout the system in positive ways. In most system diagrams, there are one to three key leverage points which, taken together, will influence the entire system. This means that, rather than try to focus on 15 or 20 or 25 indicators, there are a handful of indicators that can provide leverage for changing the entire system. Few of us are trained in or given to thinking in the perspective of systems. Therefore, it is often surprising to the group to discover which are the key leverage indicators.

- Indicators with many connections are deeply embedded in the system as it is understood today by the stakeholders and can likely be influenced by a wide range of actions.
- Indicators with few connections are relatively peripheral to the system and may require specially focused efforts to influence them.

Indicators with many arrows coming into them are likely to change as a result of actions focused on other indicators. We call these **key results indicators**.

They are not the places to begin to change the system; rather they are the areas where we would expect to see change over time if our assumptions about the influence of the key leverage indicators are correct. These are downstream indicators.

The group should emerge from the indicator analysis with a goal, a list of no more than 3–4 key leverage indicators prioritized based on their strength, a list of 1–2 key results indicators and a list of key assumptions related to the leverage indicators and results indicators. This is a compact, yet immensely powerful set of information that the participants are now armed with, after about a day of work, which will be used as the foundation of their work over the entire course of their efforts to work towards their shared goals.

The results of an indicator analysis are often surprising to the group that did the work. It can even seem like magic! But the analysis itself provides a record of how the results emerged that can be reviewed by participants with the help of the Measurement Guide if needed.

Here is an example of an indicator analysis completed by a group working to develop a scenic byway (see Figure 6.4).

Goal: **Byway visitors are exposed to a one-of-a-kind biological and geological ecosystem.**

The two strongest key leverage indicators that emerged from this analysis were #10 with 10 solid arrows connecting it with other indicators, and #5, with 7 solid arrows connecting it with other indicators. Every other indicator in the system is touched by at least one of these two, meaning that, if the assumptions present during the analysis are correct, working to move just

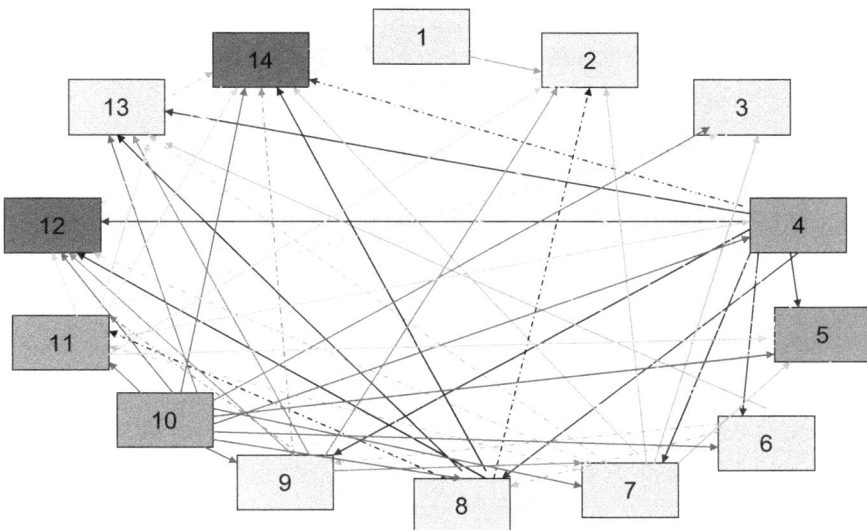

Figure 6.4 Byways indicator analysis

these two indicators in the correct direction will move ALL the indicators in the right direction. The strength of these indicators is apparent through the prevalence of solid lines. Often key leverage indicators exert influence through a combination of solid and dotted lines, and those with more solid lines are considered stronger.

> Indicator #10 was: Increase in number of visiting school groups.
>
> Indicator #5 was: Increase in local media coverage that focuses on the uniqueness of the area.

The key results indicators, with many arrows coming into them, were numbers 12 and 14.

> Indicator #12 was: Increased questions asked by visitors at the visitors' centre.
>
> Indicator #14 was: Growth of private tour operator businesses.

Based on the analysis performed by this group of stakeholders, positive changes in indicators #10 and #5 would drive positive changes in indicators #12 and #14 over time and would also drive the entire system closer to the goal.

An indicator analysis should be completed for each priority goal. Once key leverage indicators are identified for each goal, it can be helpful to view them as a suite and look for any areas of potential conflict. For example, a group has two goals:

> #1 Our economic base is diverse.
>
> #2 We have a clean environment.

The key leverage indicator for goal #1 is *reducing the cost of energy for manufacturers*. There are many possible ways to do this, some of which would have an adverse impact on the natural environment, while others would not. In considering the effects of a change in this indicator on goal #2, the group may wish to reframe the indicator to specify no adverse effects on the natural environment. The reframed key leverage point might become *reducing the cost of energy for manufacturers without degrading the natural environment*. This will help to ensure that the group is not working at cross purposes and that efforts made to achieve one goal do not undermine progress toward another.

Stakeholder participants are often surprised to see which indicators emerge as key leverage indicators. For example, in 2009, a group of stakeholders in West Virginia decided that they wanted to support the local food system. They decided that the way to do that was to start a programme in horticulture at the local university. They were working with a regional consultant who had recently completed training to become a Measurement Guide and she suggested that they go through the YGWYM process before taking any action.

About 10 stakeholders came together including staff of the West Virginia Community Development Hub, one of their funders, and a representative from the university. Their goal was to develop a strong local food system. The key leverage indicator that emerged from their analysis was *not* a programme in horticulture at the local university. It was 'more demand for local food'. This was the indicator that would drive the entire system of indicators toward a strong local food system.

The results of the YGWYM analysis completely changed the direction of the initiative. Instead of pouring time and resources into a horticulture programme at the local university, the Community Development Hub and other stakeholders chose to educate consumers about the availability, accessibility, and benefits of local food. The funder supported a programme to double the value of food assistance money used to buy fresh local vegetables. Farmers' markets began displaying signs comparing the cost of local food to food purchased in the grocery store to counter the perceptions that local products were unaffordable. This all came about due to the shift in focus because of the YGWYM process. Today, the focus is moving to the supply side, since demand has now outstripped it.[1] One of the partners in this effort, the West Virginia Food Hub, originally made funding decisions by simply asking communities what they want; now, however, they require communities to explain how they will know if they are making progress toward their goals.

In contrast to the key leverage indicators, once the analysis is completed, the key results indicators generally appear to be relatively obvious to the group. For example, in a Becoming a Measurement Guide[2] training in 2019 attended by practitioners from St Thomas and St Croix in the Caribbean, one goal developed was '**We are a community where our unique culture includes everyone**.'

The key leverage indicators, in order of strength, were:

1. *All our cultures including Moslems, Jews, native people, descendants of colonizers, and more are recognized and respected.*
2. *More people in our community participate in annual cultural events and activities.*
3. *The paradigm shifts to include culture as a foundation for all aspects of education.*
4. *The education system includes the languages of the island cultures.*

The key results indicator with arrows coming in and none going out, was:

Fewer people will be left out of participation in the tourism industry.

By moving the key leverage indicators in the desired direction, if the groups' assumptions are correct, over time they would expect to see the result. The group agreed that the key leverage indicators were 'upstream' of the downstream result. They would not achieve greater inclusivity in the tourism economy without moving the key leverage indicators first.

Interpreting dotted lines and orphan indicators

Analysing indicators reveals the limitations in our knowledge and understanding of how different indicators are related and how the system works. Whenever a dotted line appears in an indicator analysis, it is because the stakeholders either perceived a weak connection between the two indicators or they could not agree about whether there was a connection at all. By looking carefully at where the dotted lines appear, stakeholders can gain a sense of where more information and/or research is needed to better understand the whole system.

Sometimes the entire analysis is filled with dotted lines. If this happens, it is a sign that the group needs more information about the system before they determine what they need to do and what they need to measure. Under these circumstances, the next step would be to create information-gathering assignments and set a date to return and share what they have learned. Then they can redo the indicator analysis integrating their new knowledge. If key leverage indicators are connected to the system predominantly through dotted lines, that is also a reason to gather more information before proceeding.

Orphan indicators are indicators with no arrows either coming out of them or coming into them from other indicators in the system. Orphan indicators are not integrated into the system as it is understood by the stakeholders. They may be part of another system related to a different goal. The Measurement Guide may suggest including orphan indicators from one indicator analysis in the analysis for a different goal if appropriate.

Capturing the results of the indicator analysis

We have developed two ways to capture the results of indicator analyses. These are relatively low-tech solutions that do not require subscribing to (or paying for) a service or a database of information that is externally maintained. One uses PowerPoint to replicate the analysis. This provides a visual representation that can help participants remember how they were thinking at the time. It can also be used to demonstrate the process to others.

The example shown in Figure 6.5 in PowerPoint replicates the analysis that was completed on flip chart paper with coloured markers and sticky notes (as described above). Each indicator has a border of a different colour that matches the colour of the arrows drawn from it to other indicators. The key leverage indicators are filled with the colour that corresponds to their arrows and labelled according to their strength as KLI 1, KLI 2, and KLI 3. The key results indicator is also filled with colour and labelled KRI. The goal should always be included on the same slide as the indicator analysis.

The same analysis is presented in Figure 6.6 in Excel. The advantage of the Excel format is that it can be used to easily record the number as well as the types of arrows between each indicator. This makes it easy to

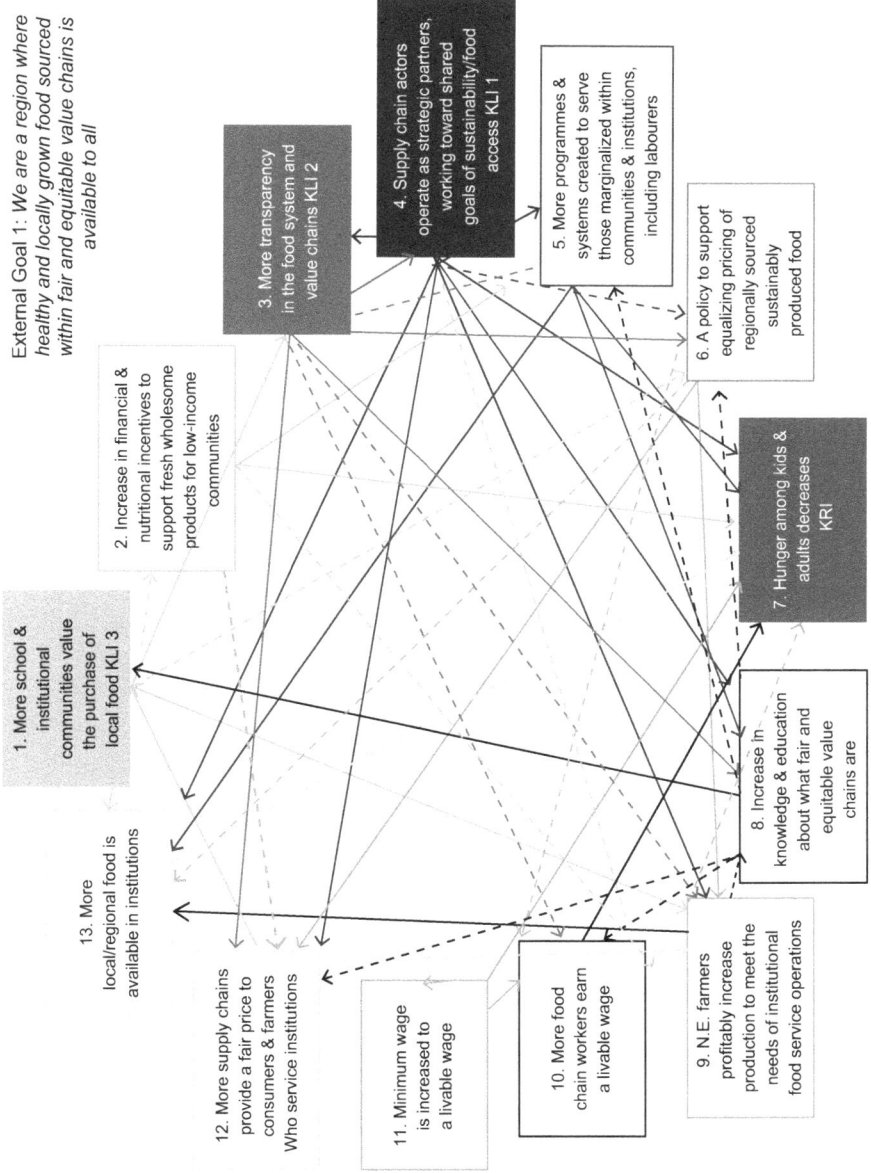

External Goal 1: *We are a region where healthy and locally grown food sourced within fair and equitable value chains is available to all*

3. More transparency in the food system and value chains KLI 2

4. Supply chain actors operate as strategic partners, working toward shared goals of sustainability/food access KLI 1

5. More programmes & systems created to serve those marginalized within communities & institutions, including labourers

6. A policy to support equalizing pricing of regionally sourced sustainably produced food

2. Increase in financial & nutritional incentives to support fresh wholesome products for low-income communities

7. Hunger among kids & adults decreases KRI

1. More school & institutional communities value the purchase of local food KLI 3

8. Increase in knowledge & education about what fair and equitable value chains are

13. More local/regional food is available in institutions

12. More supply chains provide a fair price to consumers & farmers Who service institutions

11. Minimum wage is increased to a livable wage

10. More food chain workers earn a livable wage

9. N.E. farmers profitably increase production to meet the needs of institutional food service operations

Figure 6.5 Indicator analysis in PowerPoint

External Goal #1: 20% of Vermont's transportation heating and electricity needs are supplied by renewable energy (by 2020).

Goal # / Indicators	1	2	3	4	5	6	7	8	9	10	11	12	Dotted out	Solid out	Total out	Key Leverage Indicator
1 — A majority of VT schools are heated with biomass.	D	S							S		S	S	0	3	3	
2 — More EV charging stations & cost mechanisms to encourage electric vehicle usage and make it more convenient.		S	S			S			S		S	S	0	3	3	
3 — Strong partnership between EV salespeople and renewable installers (leading to all EV using renewables to power the vehicle).	S	S			S	S	S		S		S	S	0	5	5	
4 — Transmission is built to accommodate renewable energy (not reliability).									S		S	S	0	3	3	
5 — Clear and viable permitting and siting process for renewable energy projects (biomass, wind and solar).			S	S					S		S					
6 — More vermonters (and legislators) are more comfortable understanding the benefits of renewable installations and installing renewable energy (including community renewable energy projects).							S		S		S	S	0	6	6	KLI #3
7 — Solar and wind are more visible in Vermont's working landscape				S		S			S		S	S	1	3	4	
8 — Utility rates include EV and heating options (structures)									S		S	S				
9 — VT's total energy portfolio shows an increase in renewables.											S	S	0	3	3	KRI #2
10 — Vermont has RPS in place and functioning (total energy)	S	S	S	S	S	S	S	S	S		S	S	1	6	7	KLI #2
11 — Statewide carbon emissions are going down.	S	S	S	S	S	S	S	S	S			S	0	10	10	KLI #1
12 — Gas tax receipts are down (less gas being used)											S		0	2	2	
Dotted In	1	0	0	0	0	0	0	0	0	0	0	1				
Solid In	1	3	2	2	1	4	6	1	8	0	11	6				
Total In	2	3	2	2	1	4	6	1	8	0	11	7				
Key Results Indicator									KRI #2		KRI #1					

KRI #1 = Key Results Indicator #1
KRI #2 = Key Results Indicator #2
KLI #1 = Key Leverage Indicator #1
KLI #2 = Key Leverage Indicator #2
KLI #3 = Key Leverage Indicator #3
D = Dotted (Causal relationship, not very strong or clear)
S = Solid (Direct and/or strong correlation)

Figure 6.6 Indicator analysis in Excel

determine the relative strength of each indicator in terms of its potential impact on the whole system. The key leverage indicators are clearly labelled in rows that are filled with colour. The key results indicator is found in the filled column.

There are doubtless other creative ways to capture the results of the indicator analysis and newer software solutions, but these tried-and-true methods work.

Now that we have completed the indicator analysis and identified our key leverage and key results indicators and our key assumptions (those related to our key leverage indicators), we are ready to learn how to create measures that matter.

Notes

1. Personal communication with B. Wyckoff, 11 December 2019.
2. Becoming a Measurement Guide is the name of the in-person training in how to use You Get What You Measure that was provided by Yellow Wood Associates until 2020.

CHAPTER 7
Creating measures that matter

This chapter begins by drawing the **distinction between indicators and measures** and introducing **characteristics of measures that matter**. Next it will walk you through **how measures are derived from indicators** and **dimensions in measurement**, including several case studies. The second half of the chapter is devoted to describing **how measurement results can be used to support progress toward your goals**. The emphasis here is on knowing how you intend to use the results of measurement *before* you begin to measure.

What is a measure?

A measure provides a way to count or value the status of an indicator. Things may be measured in terms of 'number of', 'percentage of', 'quality of', 'frequency of', or 'rating of', to name a few. To track a measure over time, you must have a **unit** which defines what you are counting (metres, people, litres, hours, etc.) and a **baseline** which defines the value of the measure at some predetermined starting point.

The distinction between measures and indicators is *particularly important* and is glossed over in every other process of which we are aware. Indicators are expressions of value. They answer the question, 'What needs to change to make progress toward the goal?' It is important not to limit thinking about indicators by insisting they only be things that seem obviously easy to measure. This restriction squashes creativity and often leaves out the very things that make social change so challenging yet essential. When we ask people to come up with indicators, we are asking them to describe what needs to change in the world *from their perspective* to create meaningful progress.

After the indicator analysis, we are left with a small number of things that, if they change in a positive direction, will move the entire system toward the goal. Now the question is, how would we know? That is where measures come in. *Almost anything is measurable if it is defined concretely in behavioural terms.* Behavioural terms require using language that describes changes that can be observed rather than those that are invisible or implied. For example, while we cannot tell through mind-reading whether someone's attitude or understanding or perspective has changed, we can tell whether their behaviour has changed. Once we define the behaviour that suggests progress toward the goal, we can compare the behaviour we want to see with behaviours (or the consequences of behaviours) that we can observe. The YGWYM approach allows us to go beyond the things that we think are easy to measure or for which data already exists and encourages us to grapple with the true complexity of the challenges we face and then boil them down into measurable units that are directly relevant to the work we seek to accomplish. Indicators tell us what needs to change *and* the direction of change required to make progress toward our goal. Measures tell us the status of the indicator in terms that are most relevant to our goal. We will cover how to create and implement measurement plans in Chapters Eight and Nine, but first we need to understand the difference between an indicator and a measure and how measures are derived.

Here are some examples of indicators and related measures.

Indicator: There are a wider variety of organizations meeting regularly in our community.

Measure: The number of times per month that meeting sites including the town library, town hall, and church basements are used by different organizations.

Indicator: There are more ecumenical events in our community that bring people of different faiths in contact with one another.

Measure: The number of events in our community that are officially co-sponsored by more than one religious organization and attended by people of more than one faith.

Indicator: Our community receives its fair share of state assistance for vocational education.

Measure: Dollars received for vocational education on a per pupil basis in our community compared to the state average.

Indicator: More children walk or bike to school.

Measure: The percentage of children enrolled in elementary and middle school who walk or bike to school at least one day a week during the fall and spring (or when weather permits).

How do we create measures that matter?

Measures that matter focus our attention on the things we want to change (or, sometimes, on things we want to maintain). Measures that matter are relevant within the context in which we are working whether that is a family, a town, an organization, a region, a nation, or the globe. In the YGWYM process measures are crafted in context. We do not rely on pre-existing measures (although pre-existing data may be useful if relevant). We do not suggest that stakeholder groups choose a measure from a predetermined list or create a measure by matching something from list A with something from list B. Coming up with measures that matter takes more work and creativity than that.

Basic guidelines for crafting powerful measures

There are a few basic guidelines for crafting powerful measures that we have found especially helpful and even transformative.

1. *Measure 'goods' not 'bads'*. The power and psychological impact of language is important. Many things can be measured as 'bads' or as 'goods'. For example, if our indicator was 'More days with healthy air quality,' we could measure the number of days in which air quality was dangerously bad, especially for people with pre-existing conditions. Or we could measure the number of days with healthy air quality. Here is another example. If our indicator was 'More healthy weight people,' we could measure the proportion of a population that is obese, or we could measure the proportion of the population living at a healthy weight. If our indicator was 'More people who are released from prison integrate successfully into society,' we could use the recidivism rate as the main measure or we could measure the proportion of ex-inmates that go on to be productive members of society.

   Given a choice, we should always try to measure the thing we want more of – in these three instances that would be days of healthy air quality, people living at a healthy weight, and the proportion of ex-inmates that go on to become productive members of society. Why? Because as agents of social change we always want to focus on what we really want. We could reduce the number of days with dangerous air quality without necessarily increasing the number of days with excellent air quality, and we could decrease the proportion of a population that is obese without necessarily increasing the proportion living at a healthy weight. We could reduce recidivism without increasing the number of ex-inmates who go on to be productive members of society. To stay focused on the 'good' we need to articulate our measures in terms of 'goods' not 'bads'.

   Since measures serve to focus our attention and ultimately guide our actions, we should focus on desired outcomes. Otherwise, we will build systems that are always focused on producing fewer 'bads' and never focused on producing more 'goods'. There is always more to producing a 'good' outcome than simply avoiding a 'bad' outcome.

2. *Measure only those things that will give needed information*. Keep the measures as simple as possible given the complexities of the situation. Only be as accurate as you need to be. Accuracy to the fourth decimal place is unlikely to matter. Measures of social change developed through YGWYM should provide evidence of the direction and relative magnitude of change; they are not intended as a substitute for laboratory measures or measurements produced from econometric models. Make sure the results of your measures will give you the information you need to make better decisions. Avoid measuring for its own sake.[1] (See the story in Chapter Two about measuring the turbidity of water in a stream as an illustration of degrees of precision in measurement.)

3. *Know how you will use the results of measuring before you measure.* Too much energy currently goes into collecting data that is neither useful nor used. Avoid adding to the waste. The first step is to be sure that you know how you will use the information you collect *before* you decide to collect it. (See Chapter Eight for more on this.)

4. *Balance the need to know with the ability to find out.* In my 35+ years of research experience, I have found that the things we assume will be easy to find out often turn out to be much more difficult than we imagined and, conversely, the things we think will be difficult to find out can turn out to be surprisingly straightforward, especially if we are able to identify the appropriate information gatekeeper. (More on this in Chapter Eight.) Since resources are always limited, if you stick with what you really need to know (not what would be 'nice' to know) and take into account the other guidelines, you can often avoid going down rabbit holes that require more time and resources than is warranted by the value of the information gained.

5. *Use measurement to intentionally test your assumptions.* Remember the assumptions you identified as part of your indicator analysis? These are the assumptions which, if they are incorrect, would cast doubt on your entire systems analysis. When you craft your measures, consider whether and how they will help you test those assumptions.

Keep these basic guidelines in mind as you craft measures to monitor the status of your key leverage indicators.

Defining key leverage indicators in measurable terms

Key leverage indicators describe the most powerful places that need to change in the system you have defined to make progress toward the goal. The first step in creating a measure of the status of a key leverage indicator is to define it in relation to your goal. This step in the YGWYM process provides additional focus and clarity.

The definitions you craft will not be dictionary definitions; rather they will define your key leverage indicator in behavioural terms in relation to your goal. What are the behavioural changes you would have to see to know that progress is being made toward the goal? What changes in conditions or behaviour are observable? If you cannot see it, you cannot measure it. If you would not know it if you saw it, you will not be able to think clearly about how to bring it about.

The goal should be posted and visible to all participants as they engage in defining the key leverage indicator.

If the goal is '**Our state is virus free**' and a key leverage indicator is '**Everyone who has been exposed to the virus quarantines**', the terms that need to be defined to create a measure include 'exposed to the virus', 'everyone', and 'quarantines'. The Britannica Dictionary defines quarantine as 'the period of time during which a person or animal that has a disease or that might have a disease is kept away from others to prevent the disease from spreading'.[2] This definition is far too vague to be useful from a measurement perspective. Compare this to the definition of quarantine used by the State of Vermont with respect to COVID-19.

> Quarantine applies to people with no symptoms who were 1) in close contact with someone sick with COVID-19, or 2) are returning to Vermont from out of the state (except select counties) for anything other than an essential purpose. They must stay home. They may not go outside unless they are completely alone. They may not go to work or go grocery shopping. These conditions apply for fourteen days. If symptoms appear during quarantine, they must move from quarantine into isolation. They may get tested during the quarantine period, and if results are negative, they may end their quarantine.[3]

This definition is context specific and behavioural. It makes it clear what 'counts' as quarantine and what does not 'count'.

To craft a measure, you would need to continue by defining what counts as 'exposed to the virus' and who you mean by 'everyone'. For example, does 'everyone' include people who have already recovered from COVID-19? Does it include people who have been vaccinated? Once you have defined these terms, you will know exactly what you are trying to count. You will have defined the relevant unit of measure. You will only be counting those instances that fit the criteria of your unit of measure. That is what counts; all the rest is noise.

Only when you have arrived at behavioural definitions and you clearly understand your unit of measure, should you consider how to best go about gathering the needed data. *This is a radical approach*. The more typical approach is to begin with the data at hand and pretend that it is useful, relevant, and all we need to know to make better decisions. That is almost never the case. When you begin instead by defining key leverage indicators in behavioural terms in relation to the goal, you reinforce the vision of what needs to change to make progress and you discover the information you really need to make better decisions, some of which may be different from what you might have imagined based on the limits of available data and your own mental models, which have been shaped by existing systems.

The YGWYM process is your chance to get clear about what you really need to know - not what would be nice or interesting to know, because that could go on forever - but what you *really need to know* to make better decisions that will move you toward your goal. This is your chance to break out of the limitations that come from thinking that you must use the data that already exists and that you are aware of and instead think about the data you really need to make better decisions, whether or not you think it currently exists. (You may be surprised to find it already does, but you will never know if you do not see the value in searching for it.)

Defining the terms in the key leverage indicator offers the opportunity to make even the most abstract concepts concrete in the context of your goal. As a Measurement Guide (a facilitator of the YGWYM process), once you know this, you can assure participants that they do not need to concern themselves with how their indicators will be measured when they first articulate them. The bridge from indicators to measures is crossed through defining terms in context and the context is better understood after the indicator analysis is completed. Just as the process of coming up with indicators of progress revealed the range of meaning participants attribute to the goal; the process of defining indicators in measurable terms helps create a shared sense of what really matters.

Box 7.1 The power of measures in aligning actions with goals: an example from the field

Here is how the process played out for a food hub in Michigan, as relayed by the Director at the time.

> I had been hired as a contractor to turn the food hub around, and eventually I became the Director. I got contacted by the Wallace Center about participating in a study of food hubs asking if I had the time. I blew it off. They called again and I reluctantly agreed to participate. It turned out to be one of the best things that ever happened to us. We were offered the opportunity to work with Yellow Wood and YGWYM. We had just moved to a new facility. We went from 4,000 sq. ft to 16,000 sq. ft.

This was around 2011 and local food was not on people's radar in our area. The local food system had pieces missing in infrastructure, marketing, and education. The first part of our instructions from you guys was to bring in our community partners. That was the first really brilliant thing about the process. It gave us community buy-in. We had the schools, food pantry, Good Will, food service people, restaurateurs, farmers, Chamber of Commerce, representatives from the culinary school at the community college. The owner of a large agri-tourism destination and more. We had a really good turnout, maybe 30–35 people. When we started, we had no common language, no accepted way to talk about the benefits of local food across the board, including health, jobs, and the local economy.

We worked over two days. The first day we identified our goals and indicators and did the indicator analysis. The second day was honing in and figuring out our measures and actions.

Once we completed the analysis, we narrowed our indicator list from ten major topics to three: education, food safety, and mission. These were the three to push on to move our entire system toward the goal of a strong local food system. We discovered that our strongest key leverage indicator

---

(Continued)

Box 7.1 Continued

related to education was for our food hub to become the go-to organization for everything about local foods and farming. If you are a farmer and you want to know how to get your food into a local market, you call us. If you are a restaurant looking for asparagus, you call us. If you are concerned about how to handle food safety or you have concerns about food safety, you call us.

We decided that the measure of progress for this key leverage indicator would be how often the food hub was asked to make a presentation or a speech or participate in a panel discussion. It was not hard to establish a baseline, because at that time, we were not asked very often. The first action we took was to train seven key employees, including me in public speaking. Our local community college has tremendous resources, and we found a trainer there.

We each had to work on making a speech that was directly related to our work and mission. We were each making a speech a week for about four weeks on the strength of our mission and impact on our community. We were making the speeches internally. Everyone got really good at telling the story. And everyone in the organization heard the story over and over again. List the things, tell them what you're going to tell 'em, tell 'em, tell 'em what you told 'em. It is a very effective method. We had all the department heads get trained in speech making. Each head talked about their own work. The Farm to School person talked about the impact on school gardens, nutrition, etc. We were touching on multiple areas within our realm of expertise. We had Sales, Purchasing, Farm to School, Warehouse Manager, Operations Manager, and me all making speeches.

I do not remember the number of times we were asked to speak after that, but it certainly went up from the baseline and it wasn't long before we were being recognized across the state. Word of what we were doing kept spreading. The training in public speaking engrained the mission and embedded everything into our organizational culture. We were growing 50% a year. Over the next few years, we grew from 5 employees to 60 and from $400,000 in sales to $8 million. You cannot experience that type of organizational growth without a serious cultural nurturing based on core beliefs and values. Everyone could speak to it, everyone spoke the same language and used the same words. The value internally was incalculable. We even got invited to the White House.

I think more than anything what YGWYM did was taught the management team to ask questions about the impact both upstream and downstream of the things we were doing. It really focused on making sure the number of unintended consequences were as minimal as we could make them. It is fascinating when you have the culture created where it is second nature for people to mentally do that exercise. We got there.[4]

Order of operations

The order in which you define the terms in the key leverage indicator matters. In general, it works best to begin with the nouns, followed by verbs, and then modifiers (adjectives and/or adverbs). The definition of the nouns tells you what you are talking about, while the definition of the verbs tells you what the actions are that interest you. Defining modifiers lets you become even more specific about what you will count. Let us go back to our example where the goal is 'We have a strong local economy' and the primary key leverage indicator is 'More spending by residents.'

The first question is, 'What do you mean by "residents"?' The definition of resident clarifies who will be counted and who will not. That decision should be made by considering who needs to be counted so that the key leverage point will impact the entire system as intended. The idea is to be no more inclusive than necessary; just inclusive enough to make it work. Depending on the nature of the community, for example, it could be important to include 'daytime residents' or commuters and possibly business owners who do not necessarily live locally. In some communities, it might be important to include second homeowners or seasonal residents or students. On the other hand, if the community is not in an area that attracts visitors and/or is not a place that a significant number of people travel to for their jobs or schooling, it may be sufficient to define 'residents' as people who maintain a mailing address or who pay residential property taxes in the community. Depending on the demographics of the community, it may be important to include spending by children and teens as well as adults. *The discussion should be about how narrow the definition can be while still having the anticipated impact on the system that will drive progress toward the goal.* Remember, this is not about coming up with dictionary definitions. Abstract answers will not be helpful; look for meaningful definitions that are context specific.

The second word to define is the verb 'spending'. What is 'spending' in the context of making progress toward the goal? Is it just money, or are you including spending of time and energy? Are you most interested in the overall amount of spending, or is there a particular type of spending that is most important? Perhaps the type of spending that really matters is spending on services or perhaps it is spending on goods. Possibly, to have the intended impact, spending is not just about purchasing things but also charitable contributions. Again, this needs to be determined in the context of the situation and in relation to the goal.

The last word to consider is the modifier 'local'. What is 'local'? Here too, the point is to craft a definition that drives the system toward the goal and is focused and not overly inclusive. Once you have defined the terms in the key leverage indicator, you have the information you need to derive a unit of measure and a baseline.

Units and baselines

A **unit of measure** gives you your standard of measurement. It is the amount by which you are counting. For example, if you were measuring a football field, your unit of measure would probably be yards. Yards are the measure used in determining progress in football games. The units used in measuring key leverage indicators related to social change are generally more complex.

As an example, let us assume the terms in the indicator 'More local spending by residents' were defined as follows:

Dollars paid by people, including children and young adults, who have permanent residences in and within a 20-mile radius of X town, to locally owned retail and wholesale businesses in and within a 20-mile radius of X community.

Given this definition, the **unit of measure**, or the things that would be counted, would be dollars spent in locally owned businesses by local people as defined. Dollars spent by others would not count. Dollars spent at businesses that were not locally owned would not count. *The unit must include all elements of the definition.*

Baseline measures provide the status of the indicator at a point in time before you take intentional action to move it in the desired direction. The **baseline** would be the *dollars paid by people, including children and young adults, who have permanent residences in and within a 20-mile radius of X town to locally owned retail and wholesale businesses in and within a 20-mile radius of X community*, currently or at some time in the past for which data is available. The baseline should always be established before actions are taken to move the indicator in the desired direction; otherwise, there is no beginning to your story. When historical data does not exist, the baseline is established the first time you measure. (See Chapter Eight for more on how to implement measures.)

Changing measures, changing mindsets

The application of YGWYM can lead to new insights into which measures are most powerful. For example, the US Forest Service's Cooperative Forestry Unit applied YGWYM to develop measures toward its goals, one of which was 'Sustainable natural resources with multiple benefits.' One of the programme areas relevant to this goal is the Conservation Easement Legacy Program and one of the key leverage indicators of progress toward the goal was 'more conserved acres'.

In the early 2000s when the original YGWYM sessions occurred, the preferred method for measuring the impact of conservation was the number of acres to which easements had been applied. This was calculated on a deal-by-deal basis. However, it became clear through stakeholder interaction during the YGWYM analysis that a more powerful measure would be the amount of potential development taken off the table at the landscape level (across ownerships) when development rights are purchased. Initially, there was a great deal of pushback from stakeholders who were not part of the YGWYM sessions against using this measure. One reason given was that the information would be too difficult to acquire. Another was based on resistance to adopting a landscape level versus a parcel-by-parcel approach. Eventually, about 15 years later, a new Deputy Chief for State and Private Forestry came along who saw the value in landscape level measures. He worked inclusively for over three years and engaged hundreds of people and dozens of committees and eventually achieved buy-in to landscape level measures. Today, the landscape level focus is reflected in legislation and the measure is well accepted. The obstacle was not the availability of information (which was not difficult to obtain) but rather the mindsets of practitioners. The new Deputy Chief was successful, in part, because a core group of practitioners already understood and supported the rationale for the new measure. Collecting and analysing data at the landscape level allows practitioners to identify parcel level targets for future conservation that will fulfil specific landscape level functions like maintaining wildlife corridors.

Dimensions in measurement

Measures can be amazingly simple, relatively complex, or somewhere in between. Measures increase in complexity depending on the number and types of dimensions they include.

There are four types of dimensions that are worth considering when you are defining measures of social change. Every measure does not have to include every dimension. Your measures should be only as complex as they need to be to give you the information you really need to make better decisions about how to make progress toward your goal. Anything else is likely to lead to a waste of resources and should be considered extraneous, even if it is 'what we've always done'.

1. The number of qualifiers in a unit of measure

> Example: If your goal is 'We are a community with prosperous family farms,' and your key leverage indicator is 'More sales of regionally produced meats,' one measure of progress might be 'the number of wholesale buyers of regionally produced meat'. You might choose a limited definition of 'meat' as beef, and a limited definition of 'wholesale buyer' to only include anyone that buys meat for further sale to restaurants. You might define 'regional' as within 50 miles of the community.

If it is important to your goal to have more information, your measure will need to include more specific qualifiers.

> Example: If you were to define 'wholesale buyer' to include several distinct categories such as processors and distributors who sell to institutions as well as restaurants, and 'regional' to include several concentrated population centres that you wish to target, and 'meat' to mean 'beef, chicken, turkey, and pork', the measure becomes more complex. You will need to collect more, and more precise information, which will take additional effort.

Qualifiers determine the information you will need and the degree of precision in your measure. The measures you use should be no more precise than necessary to improve the quality of your decision-making. *There is no point in spending precious resources gathering information you are unable or unlikely to use.* This is where it is particularly important to distinguish what might be nice to know from what you really need to know to make better decisions.

2. Creating a measure that compares one quantity to another

The information you really need to make better decisions may not be a single quantity, but rather the relationship between two quantities.

> Example: Perhaps the measure that matters is the proportion of meat purchased by wholesale buyers that is identified as a local or regional product. When a measure is framed as a proportion, a percentage, or a ratio, it is essentially comparing one quantity to another. Even simple comparisons can be immensely helpful in understanding the bigger picture. (See information about framing measures in Chapter Eight.)

3. Measuring across different spheres of impact

Depending on the nature of your goal and key leverage indicator, you may want to know how a change in one aspect of an indicator affects and is affected by other aspects. For example, you may want to explore the relationship between a change in an economic dimension to a change in a social or environmental dimension.[5]

> Example: Suppose one of your goals is 'We have a strong regional food system,' and another high priority goal is 'We have a healthy natural environment.' Now suppose the key leverage indicator for the first goal is 'more sales of regionally produced meat'. In defining the terms in the indicator to arrive at a measure, you may choose to look at the proportion of regionally produced meat that is organic or free range (or some other proxy for environmentally benign or beneficial), to all regionally produced meat. This allows you to learn about environmental impacts as well as overall production (and can serve as a framing measure. For more about framing measures, please see Chapter Eight).

> Here is another example: Suppose one of your goals is 'People who work in our community can afford to live here,' and one key leverage indicator is 'Businesses that employ people who live in our community pay a living wage.' You may choose to define 'living wage' in terms of the cost of housing in your community. While this adds complexity to the measure, it will likely reveal information more pertinent to your goal than simply knowing wage level paid by local businesses and businesses that employ local people. Again, the point is not to add

complexity for its own sake, but only if it will help you better understand and make decisions about how to make progress toward the goal.

4. The time factor

Time is a critical dimension in measurement as it is in systems thinking in general. A good systems thinker takes into consideration the time it takes for information to travel through a system and for feedback to result in change. Measuring over time helps identify trends while using time as a dimension of measures may establish duration and help identify other important patterns.

> Example: It takes three data points to establish a trend. Therefore, if you measure 'the number of wholesale buyers of regionally produced meat' once a year for three years, you can see the trend (or lack thereof). However, purchasing patterns may also be seasonal. If it would help you to understand the patterns of purchase over the course of the year, you might need to measure monthly for several years. The choice of time frame for your measure can be built into its definition and should be related to the actions you choose to take to move the measure in the desired direction and the time frame within which you imagine change can come about. You will learn more about this as your work continues, and it is useful to start with an explicit assumption about when you would expect to see measurable changes.

Now that we have discussed how to derive measures from key leverage indicators, it is time to talk about the different ways in which the information you gain through measuring can be used. We introduce this topic before discussing how to implement measures on the ground because, **if you do not know how you are going to use information before you collect it, you should not be collecting it**. Collecting information when you do not know how you will use it is often a feature of extractive data collection processes. Of course, your use of the information may change depending on what you learn, but you should take the time to think through several possibilities *before* you begin the process of collecting data. This will help you zero in on the most important information to collect and it will help you make choices as to how to collect it.

Begin at the end

Stephen Covey, in his book *The 7 Habits of Highly Effective People*, talks about the importance of beginning at the end with a clear destination in mind based on what really matters to us. YGWYM does this by focusing our attention on the goal we are seeking to achieve. It is our focus on the goal that allows us to identify key leverage indicators and get from there to relevant measures of progress.

Considering how we expect to use the information we collect at the outset has several advantages. First, it allows us to explain to others what we are doing and why. Clear explanations go a long way toward eliciting positive engagement. Second, it allows us to match the way we collect information to the use(s) to which we intend to put it. Third, it helps guard against the tendency to collect information for its own sake and/or collect more information than we have the capacity to put to good use.

There are at least three distinct ways to use the measurement information in relation to social change, and they are not necessarily mutually exclusive. First, measurement should always be used to **learn about what is and is not changing as a result, at least in part, of actions that you and others are taking**. Part of this learning has to do with **testing your assumptions**. One of the assumptions you should test has to do with how long it will take to make change. It is easy to be wrong in both directions: sometimes things change much more rapidly than you may have thought possible, and at other times the opposite may be true. Part of the work of social change is learning what is possible in a given time frame and how to build the feedback loops into a system that can shorten the time it takes to induce change.

Secondly, the results of measurement may also be used to help you make progress toward your goals by **educating others**. Thirdly, you may wish to use the results to **influence key decision-makers**. The YGWYM process provides a context for the information collected through each measure that is logical and compelling. Presenting the results of measurement should begin with recalling the goal, the key leverage indicators, and the measures, including baselines and framing measures and then moving on to the results of (re-) measurement. The tools introduced in Chapter Six regarding how to capture the results of the indicator analysis can be quite helpful in this regard.

While there is no way to know in advance what the measurement process will reveal, thinking through how you will use the results before you start collecting data can help you choose appropriate data collection tools and partners as well as ensure that you are only collecting information that will be genuinely useful in making better decisions to enact social change.

Assessing your impact

We assume that most who use YGWYM do so because they want to use the results of measurement to learn about what is and is not changing because of actions being taken to attempt to make progress toward the goal. The first step in doing this is to create a **baseline** (as discussed briefly above and later extensively in Chapter Eight). A baseline characterizes the conditions in play before intentional actions are taken to move the key leverage indicators in the desired direction. Baselines may be created using historical data if such data exists. However, it is often true that the information we need to make better decisions is NOT the information that is readily available. For example, when Partners in Health (PIH) arrived in Peru, it was widely assumed that

Peru's tuberculosis (TB) treatment programme was excellent. Yet, PIH staff kept encountering individuals who had been treated for TB multiple times and were still ill. Since the prevailing wisdom was that the existing programme was producing excellent results, no one had collected data on people with treatment resistant tuberculosis. PIH staff did that work themselves and were eventually able to administer treatment to the types of patients who had been previously allowed to die. The baseline was created by PIH as they assessed the extent of the problem.[6] It is not unusual that the types of indicators developed through YGWYM require baselines to be created the first time measurement occurs. This is because measures identified through YGWYM are context rich and often challenge prevailing wisdom (or at least provide an opportunity to test it).

Once a baseline is established, and actions are taken to move key leverage indicators in the desired direction, periodic re-measurement allows for ongoing assessment and learning that can be used to refine actions and improve impacts over time.

Educating others

If you have gone through the YGWYM process to derive your measures, what you learn by measuring will likely add new information and insights to the discussion about the system you are trying to impact. What you learn needs to be shared to help all the actors in the system understand better how it works, including but not limited to the stakeholders involved in the analysis. This is especially important if the information you gather contradicts one or more of the assumptions that your stakeholders or others are making about how to get to your goal. Even a baseline measurement can yield new and important information for decision-makers and others.

For example, Clinton County in north eastern New York State wanted to know what impact its neighbour, Canada, had on its economy. Historical data on spending, property ownership, and other aspects of the economic impact of Canadians was not available, so the baseline was established the first time we measured. The initial measures were taken at a single point in time, and before actions were taken to influence the situation; therefore they could not reveal the effectiveness or lack thereof of the actions. However, simply knowing the scale and scope of Canada's economic impact on various aspects of the Clinton County economy at the baseline was very important in getting the attention of policymakers and the general public and in generating the investment and commitment required to continue measuring as they took actions to move toward the goal of increasing positive impacts and reducing negative ones. They re-measured every 2 years for at least 12 years to track the effects of investments made in strengthening positive economic impacts. Measurement results were distributed to key stakeholders and shared with the general public, all of which contributed to increased awareness, focused investments, and positive actions.

Influencing decision-makers

You may wish to use the results of measuring to attempt to influence key decision-makers directly. For instance, in the example of the citizens concerned about the impact of turbidity linked to dam discharges on the health of their river (see Chapter Two) the citizens' group knew from the outset that they wanted to influence decision-makers. They also wanted to compel others, with greater resources and scientific expertise than the citizens had available, to investigate the relationship between stream turbidity and dam releases upstream. Although they did not have access to sophisticated scientific equipment, they recognized that they had to introduce enough rigour into their data collection process so that the results were convincing. Otherwise they knew they would not be taken seriously. They designed a replicable protocol for measurement that, though imperfect, produced data of sufficiently high quality to suggest the need for further investigation.

If your goal is 'Jobs in our region are filled by people who live here,' and your key leverage indicator is 'More affordable housing,' you might want to influence the decisions of housing developers, regulators, bankers, realtors, or owners of existing housing stock to make it easier to develop or redevelop housing stock appropriately.

An Assistant Director at the US Department of Agriculture (USDA) Forest Service wanted to encourage the use of cross-laminated timber (CLT) in the construction of buildings for its environmental and cost advantages. After experiencing YGWYM and realizing the amount of unnecessary reporting required by USDA, he convinced his bosses to let him hire a firm that specializes in collecting data on buildings. They measured the amount of carbon sequestered in every building and what was different because it was built using CLT. They also tracked the costs of construction. These measures allowed the Assistant Director to determine the return on investment on reducing greenhouse gases per dollar of federal money. Using data to influence adoption of CLT proved much more cost effective than, say, having USDA foot the costs of constructing buildings. By proving the superior return on investment of a data-driven approach to influencing the use of CLT, the programme has gained bipartisan support in Congress based on its performance.[7]

If you think you will want to use the information you gather to influence decision-makers, it is worth spending some time considering these questions before you complete your measurement plan:

a. Who has the power to reallocate resources to move your indicator in the desired direction? Here it is useful to think about the same three categories of stakeholders you considered when inviting participants into the YGWYM process, namely: 1) those who can make positive changes, 2) those who can prevent positive changes, and 3) those who would be affected by positive changes.

b. What is the time frame within which they make decisions? Is it when they pass an annual budget; does it pertain to voting on a particular piece of legislation, or is there no definite time frame? If you are targeting a specific decision, it is critical to design your measurement plan so that you will have the information you need in sufficient time to analyse, interpret, and prepare it for presentation. More than one social change group has experienced the frustration of not being able to provide useful information in a timely manner.

c. What type of information will be most compelling? Are the decision-makers you are trying to influence more interested in stories or in numbers? If you are presenting multi-dimensional measures, which dimensions will they find most compelling? Which constituencies are they most responsive to and how can you include the experiences of those constituencies in your measurements? While it is important to maintain the integrity of the measurement process by continuing to align your measures with your key leverage indicators and your goal, there may be choices you can make that will also enhance the likelihood of influencing resource allocation decisions in the direction you seek.

d. What is the best medium in which to present your information? *How you collect* the information should be influenced by what you intend to do with it, including how you expect to present it. If you intend to use the information you collect to influence decision-makers, you should consider how they will use it. Will they want a printed report? A video? Testimony? There are many ways to present information: press releases, articles in community papers and newsletters, radio spots, blogs, posters, meetings, video streams, theatre, murals, etc. Each choice may have implications for how you collect the information. If you want to produce a video, for example, that is something you need to decide early on. If you are planning to prepare the data you collect to fit into a dashboard or scorecard format that may also have implications for how you collect it. (Please see Chapter One for more about dashboards and scorecards.)

Choosing the right messenger

The messenger is the person and/or organization who communicates your findings to the decision-makers you wish to influence. Choosing the right messenger can make a big difference in how your message is received. This is particularly true when you plan to use your measurements to educate others and/or to influence decision-makers. Who are the messengers that your intended audience is most likely to find credible and compelling? This can influence who you invite to participate in the process to begin with as well as who you recruit to deliver the information. Ideally, your messenger should be one or a combination of stakeholders who have participated in the YGWYM process and are likely to be well-received by your intended audience.

The beauty of the YGWYM process is that it engages a wide range of different types of stakeholders, who, through the process, come to consensus regarding the most important things that need to change under current conditions to make progress toward their shared goal. Depending on your goal and the kind of work that needs to happen to make progress, you may have the latitude to make changes without the need to concentrate on influencing decision-makers at all. Often important changes can happen from the bottom up through community-based efforts. Participating in the process of YGWYM builds social and intellectual capital and promotes effective collaborations among stakeholders. It is useful to realize that it can also build political capital by broadening the base of constituents supporting a given change in resource allocation. The YGWYM process contributes to building the relationships required to create diverse coalitions that are difficult for decision-makers to ignore. This is true for formal and informal decision-makers at local levels as well as at higher levels of influence.

Skilled advocacy

Whether you intend to share your measurement results for the purpose of educating others or to attempt to influence decision-makers directly, the manner in which you present your results can make a big difference in how they are received. When working with your group, it is important to help them understand and even practise sharing the results of YGWYM with others in such a way as to help make progress toward their goals.

Skilled advocacy invites others into the thought processes that have led an individual or, in the case of YGWYM, a diverse group of stakeholders, to certain conclusions regarding the need for changes in behaviour, policies, and/or resource allocations to make progress toward specific goals. If you are seeking social change, you are an advocate and should recognize yourself as such. You care and you are not neutral. If you are going to succeed, you must engage others and help them see their interests in joining with you instead of opposing what you are advocating for.

Skilled advocacy invites you to view your audience not as enemies or obstacles but as people from whom you might learn something valuable that will strengthen your case. This means engaging honestly and thoughtfully. It means listening at least as much as you speak. And it means conveying openness rather than defensiveness.

Two ways of framing your conclusions can help with this.

1. *Explain the structure of your thinking.* You can do this by framing your presentation using some or all of the following phrases: 'We are advocating for X, and we would like to take you through our thought process. This is a complex issue with several critical dimensions. Our thoughts are … Our feelings are … Our assumptions are … In our experience, when X happens, Y often follows … Is our thinking clear?' The very structure of YGWYM with goals, an indicator analysis, recognizing assumptions, identifying key leverage points, and defining

terms in key leverage points to arrive at measures provides a roadmap for explaining the structure of your thinking.

2. *Ask for help in sorting out your thinking.* 'We're trying to make a decision about X, and we're leaning toward Y, but we're not sure it's the best choice. We would appreciate you helping us understand why we think or feel that it is the right way to go. Is there something that we've missed?' This framing invites skilled inquiry by others and can help them go deeper with you instead of simply rejecting your thinking out of hand. It can also help decision-makers 'own' the decisions that come later.

Now that we have talked about how you might choose to use the results of measures once you have them, it is time to discuss how to develop a measurement plan.

Notes

1. Thanks to Jim Rugh for introducing this concept and several others used here in Rugh (1992). Adaptations are the responsibility of the author.
2. <https://www.britannica.com/dictionary/quarantine#:~:text=1%20quarantine-,%2F%CB%88kwor%C9%99n%CB%8Cti%CB%90n%2F,prevent%20the%20disease%20from%20spreading>
3. Vermont Department of Health website [accessed 18 November 2020].
4. Telephone interview with E. Smith, 14 October 2019.
5. Maureen Hart's work on sustainability indicators is all about these types of compound measures (see Hart, 2006).
6. <https://bendingthearcfilm.com/>
7. Telephone interview with S. Marshall, Assistant Director US Forest Service, Cooperative Forestry Staff, 23 October 2019.

References

Hart, M. (2006) *Guide to Sustainable Community Indicators*, Sustainable Measures, West Hartford, CT.

Rugh, J. (1992) *Self-Evaluation: Ideas for Participatory Evaluation of Rural Community Development Projects*, World Neighbors, Oklahoma City.

CHAPTER 8
Developing a measurement plan

This chapter begins with some key concepts in measurement for social change including **units of measure**, **baselines**, and **framing measures**, and moves on to a discussion of **measurement plans**. It also discusses the difference between extractive and inclusive measurement processes and illustrates how the process of measurement itself can often be used both to establish baselines and move key leverage indicators in the desired direction over time. Before you begin to craft a measurement plan you need to: 1) know what you are trying to measure and 2) have considered how you will use the results of measurement (see Chapter Seven). One of the powerful features of the YGWYM process is that it embeds measures in the planning process from the start instead of adding them in as an afterthought (if at all) once actions have already been taken. The work of embedding measures begins here.

Units of measure

The first step in crafting a measurement plan is to create a unit of measure. The way you define the unit of measure for any given key leverage indicator tells you what 'counts' and what does not 'count'. Defining the unit of measure is the key to moving from a values-based statement about what needs to change to say that progress is being made toward the goal, an indicator, to a measure that tells you what exactly needs to change and how you will know. This process of defining key terms in your key leverage indicators is the way in which otherwise abstract and sometimes seemingly unmeasurable concepts become tangible and measurable. **Remember, the relevant definitions are those that connect your key leverage indicator to the goal; not the definitions you would find in a dictionary**.

Early in its organizational development, the Vermont Environmental Consortium[1] (VEC) used YGWYM to establish goals, one of which was, **Vermont's environment-related business, agencies, and educational institutions exist within a closely networked, collaborative community of reciprocal support**.

The most powerful key leverage indicator (with the strongest connections to other indicators in the system) was **VEC initiates direct communication to academic faculty and staff about training opportunities, research opportunities, and internship opportunities with VEC members**.

Three aspects of this indicator needed to be defined to create the unit of measure. These were:

- VEC initiates;
- direct communication;
- training, research, and internship opportunities identified with VEC members.

'VEC members' were readily definable as dues-paying members. 'Academic faculty and staff' were also readily definable as individuals employed by one of Vermont's institutions of higher education.

'VEC initiates' was defined as actions that began with VEC. This meant that, for example, incoming inquiries did not count. Direct communication meant either face to face, telephone, or email. It did not include things like putting posters up on campuses or posting information on the VEC website. The stakeholders who crafted the measurement plan decided that direct communication from VEC to academic staff and faculty would be the most impactful way to move their indicator in the direction of their goal. Direct outgoing communication was the focus of their measure. The only opportunities that counted were those identified by VEC members. Members could determine what constituted an opportunity in training, research, and/or internships.

Direct contact is more powerful than, for example, putting up posters on campuses or sending emails. So, putting all the pieces together, the only things that counted were opportunities identified by VEC members that were directly communicated by VEC to academic faculty and staff. This measure makes it clear which activities count and which do not and helps focus resources on the things that are most likely to lead to desired behavioural changes over the long run.

As another example, a group working on issues related to education came up with a goal stated as, '**Forty percent of our residents age 25+ have a baccalaureate degree**.' One of the key leverage indicators was '**College is more affordable for all people**.' The terms that needed to be defined included 'college', 'affordable', and 'all people'.

The group defined 'all people' as people of any race, gender, or class who were residents in their area and who qualified for college by having either a high school diploma or a General Educational Development (GED) test, including returning students with the intent to complete a degree. 'College' was defined as two or four year and public and private as well as programmes that provide a pipeline into college. 'Affordable' meant total cost including the opportunity cost of lost income, books, tuition, childcare, and transportation in relation to ability to pay.

Taken together, the measure was the total cost, including the opportunity cost of lost income, books, tuition, childcare, and transportation in relation to ability to pay, of two year and four year and college pipeline programmes in relation to the ability to pay of people of any race, gender, or class who were residents in their county and who qualified for college by having either a high school diploma or a GED, including returning students with the intent to complete a degree. If you were not a county resident, you did not count. If you did not qualify for college, you did not count. If you were seeking a non-college education, you did not count.

One term that came up while refining the measure was 'ability to pay'. The group needed to define this term before they could implement their measure. This is an example of a relatively complex measure that compares one quantity with another. The need for this level of complexity became clear in the process of defining the terms in the key leverage indicator in relation to the goal.

The same basic process of defining the terms in the key leverage indicator can be used to define and then measure more complex concepts such as the stocks of multiple forms of wealth required for an inclusive and sustainable economy. These include social, individual, intellectual, political, built, cultural, and financial capital. For more information on how to measure stocks of multiple forms of capital, please refer to Ratner (2020: Chapter 8 – Rethinking measures of economic impact).

Establishing a baseline

Any meaningful measurement process must begin by establishing a baseline. The baseline defines the prevailing conditions before any action is taken to move the key leverage indicator in the desired direction. Sometimes, information already exists that will allow you to define historical baselines. For example, if your key leverage indicator is, '**More participation in the annual interfaith conference**' and you already had information on the number of participants in years past, you would already have a baseline of sorts through past attendance records.

However, if your goal is, '**We are a tolerant and inclusive community**', you might define the terms in your key leverage indicator more specifically. For example, suppose it made sense in the context of your community or region and in the context of your goal to define 'participation' to include youth under 18, Muslims, Catholics, Jews, Hindus, and Quakers. While you may have historical data on the overall number of attendees, it may or may not be possible to identify attendees by these categories. In this case, your baseline may be enhanced the first time you measure. Sometimes there is no relevant historical data, and the entire baseline is established the first time you measure. This was the case with the group concerned with college affordability. No one had ever collected the data they were interested in, in exactly the form they needed it. The baseline was established the first time they measured the total cost of attending the schools in their region in relation to the ability to pay of the people who they wished to count.

In other instances, again depending on the nature of your indicator, the baseline may be zero. (Remember, an indicator can indicate the desired presence of something that does not yet exist.) This was the case with the Vermont Environmental Consortium. VEC members had not yet been asked to identify training, research, and internship opportunities and VEC had not targeted outreach to academic staff and faculty and had only one academic member. In other words, at the outset, the baseline for VEC's measure was zero.

VEC's measurement plan was rather simple and was designed so that the very act of measuring would help the organization make progress toward its goal. VEC began by assembling a contact list of academic staff and faculty in Vermont in disciplines relevant to their organization. This increased their awareness of who they might direct their communications toward. Next, they invited VEC members to identify training, research, and internship opportunities. This alerted members to the priority the organization was placing on outreach to academics and encouraged members who were not already thinking about it to consider how their work could be enhanced by connections with in-state academic institutions. These conversations resulted in an 'ah-ha' moment that led to specific actions that would move the indicator in the right direction. Perhaps, the Board of Directors realized, in addition to the opportunities identified by individual members, the organization as a whole could take actions that would move the measure in the desired direction. This led the organization to prioritize the topic of environmental education for their annual conference. Organizing the conference provided a reason to reach out directly to all the academics on their list.

Upon re-measuring after two years, the Director reflected,

> Establishing this priority early on really helped because I immediately assembled an academic contact list and made regular contact on any issue of interest to that constituency. The growth in our academic membership from 1 member to 8 suggests that we have gotten on their radar in a positive way. In recent months, the planned education conference, while an uphill struggle, has served to broaden, deepen, and focus these contacts.

Approximately 60 faculty and staff became a regular part of VEC's communications.

Baseline measures can inform subsequent measurement processes and even lead to modifications in goals and/or key leverage indicators and actions. In Rubiner (2007: 2), the author describes the value of baseline data this way, 'WCI (West Central Initiative) dug deeper to find meaningful baseline data on root causes (of poverty), not just symptoms; measuring outcomes, not just output.'

Baseline measures can also help test assumptions. (For more on assumptions, please see Chapters Three and Six.) For example, WCI had assumed that ensuring that job seekers had a GED would provide substantial leverage toward the goal of having economically successful families. However, the data revealed that, when retired workers were excluded, many of the job seekers in the region already had a diploma or a GED. Increasing the number of job seekers with GEDs was not the leverage point they had assumed it to be. On the other hand, baseline data also revealed the proportion of the population in the region that was eligible to receive the Earned Income Tax

Credit (EITC) and that over a quarter of eligible families never did so. This led to a significant expansion in free assistance to families to help them claim the EITC. Re-measurement showed that the number of people filing rose by 25% and the total dollars refunded was up by US$428,000 after two years (Rubiner, 2007). This was a significant step toward the goal of families that are economically successful.

Framing measures: understanding what's possible

A framing measure is a measure of the scale or scope of the issue you are trying to address in relation to your goal. For example, if you are trying to eliminate hunger within a certain geographic area, a framing measure will tell you how many people lack adequate nutrition in that area. Framing measures put our challenges as well as what we can achieve in context. They keep us honest about the scale of the challenges we are trying to address. They prevent us from sticking our heads in the sand and claiming victory for what are often, at best, marginal contributions to a large and complex goal. How often have you heard or seen a social change group claim their success based on raw numbers of constituents served, without providing any idea of the total number at risk or in need? For example, how many times have you seen a food bank tout the number of people who have come through their doors or the number of meals it has served without providing any sense of the number of people in need and the number of meals required to meet the need in the region? Or a housing group talk about the number of people served without mentioning the total number of people with housing insecurity in their service area?

There is a pathology of systems blindness in this failure to face the scale and scope of our societal problems. I suspect it is exacerbated by our tendency to think that each organization must stand alone to demonstrate its impact so that it can continue to receive support. Organizations are anxious to demonstrate that they are having an impact to reassure funders that their contributions are being put to good use; however, without framing measures, donors and contributors have no way of knowing whether the impacts are marginal or transformational. Perhaps there is also an element of shame in recognizing that one organization can only do so much, so it is more comfortable to crow about what has been accomplished than it is to acknowledge the true scope of the challenge and admit that it is too large to tackle alone.

We have overvalued attribution – for example, 'look what we did by ourselves' – and undervalued contribution – for example, 'we helped make this happen and look how much better off we all are as a result'. This focus is understandable, given the pressure that organizations and leaders feel to stand out in the minds of funders, a feature of the system we rely on to support many social change efforts. The negative consequences of this system are substantial. The focus on attribution or being expected to be able to 'prove' the difference made by a single organization, undermines our capacity to tackle problems at scale. It disincentivizes collaboration and results in ineffective resource allocation. We end up with lots of relatively small and under-resourced organizations on one end of the spectrum, each trying to do too much by themselves, and huge organizations, often trying to do too many different things at once, at the other end. Large organizations often suffer from mission drift as they chase funding. We would often be better served by strong collaborations between organizations, each utilizing their own core competencies to make progress toward shared goals. Lifting our heads to look at the entire frame gives us a chance to broaden the partnerships we build to change systems that will ultimately make a difference at scale. Getting in the habit of using framing measures will change your perspective on your work. It will also help you honestly communicate the importance of (as well as the constraints on) the work you are doing to those who fund and support it and to the partners you will need to engage to bring about transformational change.

One of my favourite examples of the use of a framing measure to activate collaboration comes from a group trying to tackle unemployment in the inner city of Chicago. They figured out the average unemployment rate for the state and for the county and then worked out how many people in the inner-city neighbourhoods they were focused on would have to obtain and maintain employment over several years to match the average unemployment rates of the county and state. They were not striving for 100% employment; they were striving for equity. Since the unemployment rate in their neighbourhoods was substantially higher than the average of the state and the county, there was a gap that needed to be filled. They determined that about 400 people per year from their neighbourhoods would need to find and keep jobs to close the gap.

The organization that created the framing measure shared this number with others who were also concerned about employment for inner-city residents. No single organization had the resources to secure and help maintain employment for 400 people a year. However, there were many organizations in the region that shared their goal. One by one, they began to step forward. One organization was able to commit to working with 20 people, another committed to working with 5 people, and so it went until there were sufficient players to address the problem at scale. Instead of each individual organization working in a vacuum, suddenly they all became accountable to one another. Framing measures, like goals, can provide a focus for self-organizing behaviour among stakeholders.

In the example regarding EITC claims, WCI was able to use a combination of US Census data about family size, age, composition, and income to estimate the number of families in their region who would qualify. Then they used data about EITC usage published by the Brookings Institute to estimate the number who may have qualified but failed to claim and the average size their payment might be. From this, they were able to estimate that approximately 3,700 families in the region were qualified but leaving an estimated $5.5 m unclaimed each year. This was their framing measure. Even though the free assistance provided resulted in an estimated increase of $428,000 over two years, because they had a framing measure, they knew that this was less than 8% of the estimated potential. They knew this was not 'mission accomplished', and that more and possibly different actions or interventions were still needed.

Framing measures can also help us understand what equity would look like. For example, when Fahe, a federation of non-profit housing developers serving six states, was developing a wealth creation value chain[2] for affordable energy efficient housing, one of the gaps in the value chain was a lack of trained inspectors to certify the energy efficiency of housing in rural areas. Fahe collected data to determine how many trained inspectors were available in their region and, of that number, how many worked in urban versus rural areas. They discovered an imbalance that favoured urban areas on a per capita basis. Knowing these numbers allowed them to determine how many inspectors had to be trained to be able to provide an equitable level of service in rural communities.

Framing measures can inform the design of actions. A non-profit in Ohio wanted to create a value chain for wood products that was environmentally sustainable as well as inclusive of small landowners and processors. They wanted the value chain to lead to improvements in forest management practices for participants (among other things). To understand the context in which their work would begin, they chose to develop a framing measure that analysed conditions across their region of impact. Their framing measure was the percentage of forest land that was under certified forest management by type of certification for each of the five states in the Central Appalachian region (Ohio, West Virginia, Kentucky, Tennessee, and Virginia). They determined that only 39 landowners across five states had forested lands that were certified by the Forest Stewardship Council (FSC). FSC was a more demanding forest stewardship certification than the other forms in use in 2012 and included biological diversity, endangered species, forests of high conservation value, indigenous peoples' and workers' rights, and impact on local communities, and more.

Findings from the framing measure, which had not been previously calculated, allowed the value chain coordinating organization to better understand the obstacles facing landowners, especially smaller landowners, who wanted to be FSC certified but found the process either unaffordable, unmanageable or both. Since expanding certification was one of the key leverage points for a successful value chain, they decided to work with partners to establish a Center for Wood and Forest Certification at the University of Kentucky. They created group certificates to lower the barriers for small landowners. Within three years, their action had allowed an additional 10 individual landowners of relatively large acreage and 60 smaller landowners to become certified. Certification not only improved forest management practices but helped landowners access new markets.

Framing measures can also help us understand what is possible. For example, if your goal is, '**We are a community with state-of-the-art employment opportunities**' and a key leverage indicator is '**We have affordable, high quality internet service for all residents**

and businesses,' it would be useful to learn how many communities like yours in your region have already achieved affordable, high-quality internet service and how many have not. Identifying those who have, even if their systems are not everything you might wish for, helps reinforce the idea that the outcome you are seeking is possible and worth pursuing. It may also help you identify the major roadblocks to progress that will impact what you choose to measure, how you choose to act, and how you can best use the results of measurement to move toward the goal. This type of 'best practice' research, though not essential to the YGWYM process, can provide insights into what has worked in other places and may be included as an action step that also informs the framing measure. Your measurement plan should include creating one or more framing measures related to your goal. Framing measures should provide you with information about the larger context in which you are operating, beyond the scope of the individuals and groups and beyond what a single stakeholder could expect to impact directly.

The measurement plan

Once the unit of measure for your key leverage indicator(s) has been defined, the question becomes how you will collect the information you need to establish a baseline and then to re-measure. Here is where it makes sense to develop and test a measurement plan. **A measurement plan is a roadmap for what you are going to measure and how you will measure it**. It can be simple; in fact, the measurement plan should be no more complicated than it needs to be to get the job done. Do not try to do too much! Remember the difference between what you need to know and what would be nice to know and keep your focus on the former. Only measure progress toward your goal(s). Measure only those things that will give you the information you really need. Balance the need to know with the ability to find out. Measure those aspects of progress that will have the most impact on decision-making in relation to your goal(s). Your measurement plan should be tailored to the use or uses to which you hope to put the results (see Chapter Seven for more on using the results of measurement).

Keeping these things in mind, you will want to develop a measurement plan for each key leverage indicator that you plan to focus on. Remember that one of the main reasons to engage in the YGWYM process is to bring focus to your work. Do not assume that you must measure every key leverage indicator. Match the energy and resources you have to the tasks at hand, and then prioritize. Your indicator analysis will tell you which of your key leverage indicators is most influential. Start there.

A complete measurement plan should include the following information:

- goal;
- key leverage indicator;
- definition of desired change;

- assumptions;
- measure:
  - unit of measure;
  - baseline period;
  - definitions of key terms.
- framing measures/data;
- data sources;
- time frame for data collection;
- roles and responsibilities;
- communication strategy;
- reporting plan and format.

These questions are designed to help guide you through developing a measurement plan:

1. What information will be needed to establish a baseline for the period you have chosen? (Remember that, in some instances, you will be creating your own baseline the first time you measure.)
2. List possible sources of secondary information, including contact details, and the intermediaries who collect/control/generate this information. Remember that different dimensions of your measure may require different sources.
3. Will you need to collect your own primary data? If so, what methods will you use?
4. What is the time frame for gathering information for your baseline?
5. What is the time frame for re-measuring? (Make sure it is realistic. Do not plan to re-measure in six months if you think it will take two years to achieve behavioural changes.)
6. How much time and other resources will it take to gather the information? Who will do it? If they need training, how will they get it? Who will store the information and keep it safe? Who will analyse it? Who will present it back to the group, along with lessons learned through the process of collecting it? (See Chapter Ten for more information on interpreting the results of measurement.)
7. Who will coordinate the information collection process and keep all stakeholders informed of progress, roadblocks, and new opportunities that emerge?
8. How can you design and implement your measurement plan so that the very process of measuring helps move the key leverage indicator toward the goal (see below)?

Measurement plans can be succinct one-page documents, or they can be detailed multi-page roadmaps depending on the needs of the group. The process of developing a measurement plan is iterative. The plan will, almost undoubtedly, change the moment you try to implement it. You will learn as you go and that learning will inform not only your measurement plan, but your understanding of the real constraints and opportunities related to making progress toward your goal(s).

It is essential that you test your measurement plan by trying it out at a limited scale before you fully commit to it. Talk to the information providers you have identified. Test your assumptions about what information is and is not available. Then revise your plan as needed. Always remember that the purpose of measurement is to help you learn about what matters in relation to your goal, provide focus that will help you see things you might otherwise miss, and help you develop actions that are more effective in making progress toward your goal over time.

Measuring as a force for change

Instead of viewing measurement as a process that is separate from the work of social change, YGWYM views the process of collecting information as a key tool in engendering social change.

For example, when the Vermont Environmental Consortium chose to measure direct communications with academic faculty and staff in environmental fields in Vermont, they were measuring an activity that would, in and of itself, contribute to their goal of engaging academics in state-wide conversation about the quality of environmental education in the state and forging stronger ties between the education and environmental business sectors for mutual benefit. This is one example of how implementing a measurement plan contributes directly to progress toward the goal. Box 8.1 provides another example to illustrate the point.

Box 8.1 Using measurement to help reduce residential water use in Colorado

A community in Colorado recognized that water was becoming a scarce resource and wanted to find ways to help residents reduce their volume of use. Their goal was '**We are an environmentally responsible community**.' One of the key leverage indicators was '**Residential water use per capita in our community is decreasing over time**.' When the group began to consider how they would collect baseline data, the first thing they thought of was some sort of survey of residential users. This way of thinking is not uncommon. However, in short order one of the stakeholders pointed out the municipal water utility already had data on water use by households. There was no need for a survey; what they needed to do was to meet with the municipal utility to identify their shared interests in water conservation and figure out how best to work with the information already available while protecting confidentiality.

(Continued)

Box 8.1 Continued

The next part of their work had to do with the actions they could take that could result in decreased water use. One such action included allowing households to have real time information on the amount of water they were using. Until that time, residents only became aware of the amount of water they were using after the fact, when they received their monthly bills. By working toward a system of real time information, the group was 1) allowing residents to gain access to the information needed to improve their own decision-making with respect to water use; and 2) improving the accuracy of data to re-measure use rates over time to determine how much progress was or was not being made toward their goal.

Studies have shown that placing a residential water meter in plain sight, combined with price incentives to reduce water use, can lead to reductions in water use. Price incentives by themselves are insufficient; users need to have the information about how much they are using to guide and change their behaviours (Tanverakul and Lee, 2015). Simply installing a meter to measure the amount of water a household is using, contributes to a reduction in use per capita even without specific price incentives based on volume reduction. Creative measurement plans seek to embed measurement processes that will, in and of themselves, help move the key leverage indicator in the desired direction.

This is a great example of how the measurement process itself can be used to create feedback loops that change the way a system works.

There are many ways to collect information and we will discuss several of them in Chapter Nine. It is beyond the scope of this volume to provide detailed instructions on any specific methods of collecting information. You will find many sources of information on the 'how-tos' depending upon the techniques you select. However, our experience suggests that some methods of collecting information are more useful than others in generating progress toward the goal when the goal pertains to social change.

Extractive versus transformational measurement

YGWYM intentionally encourages measurement processes that are *not extractive*. An **extractive measurement process** is one that forces certain groups to provide information to satisfy other groups. The information that is supplied may or may not be useful to those required to supply it, and the process of supplying it may impose a financial and/or time and/or confidentiality burden on the suppliers. Extractive data collection is a top-down process in which some individuals and groups provide information (knowingly or unknowingly) that is used primarily and disproportionately to benefit others who request or demand it. Much of the data collected in the United States from internet users fits this description. Anytime one group has the power to require information from another that has no benefit to the provider, it is an extractive process that depletes the resources of the provider. The information that is collected and the results of its analysis is often not available to those who supply the raw data. Also, those who supply the data are rarely involved in any way in its interpretation. Most of the information collected in our society is based on extractive processes. This includes most of the secondary data you may choose to rely upon.

Transactional measurement processes focus on the exchange of information without any intention to change systems or to directly improve the performance of those who provide the information. Many funders, including funders who purport to engage in social change, promote what is, essentially, transactional data collection. They require their grantees to produce information in exchange for funding to meet the needs of the funders, not the needs of the grantees. Grantees often have little if any input into the type of information required by funders. Funders spend little if any of their own resources assisting grantees in setting up information or measurement systems that would truly help the grantees learn to do their work more effectively. The burden of providing information demanded by funders generally falls squarely on the shoulders of grantees, without having their input included at the forefront.

YGWYM promotes **transformational measurement processes**. Transformational measurement is neither extractive nor transactional. Transformational data collection creates feedback loops that did not previously exist. These feedback loops can change the nature of the systems in which they are inserted. Transformational data collection is designed to simultaneously benefit those who collect it while driving the entire system toward the goal. Realizing these benefits often means investing in the capacity of stakeholders to design and implement information systems that give them the information they really need to make better decisions. For example, suppose your goal was, '**We have a resilient agricultural economy**,' and one of your key leverage indicators was, '**More small and historically disadvantaged farmers achieve and maintain profitability**,' and you define 'profitability' as net income with minimal negative environmental consequences to soil, water, and air. If, instead of relying on periodic external assessments and third party certifications, funders worked with small and disadvantaged farmers to help them implement measurement systems to determine the profitability of each of their products while taking into account all relevant factors, including the value of their own labour and environmental impacts, farmers themselves would be better able to identify which products are adding to their bottom line while imposing the least external costs on the environment. Adding this information into their farming system can be transformational and can lead to increased profitability over time with increased positive environmental impacts as well as increased capacity to adjust to changing market conditions (resilience). When farmers are able to build in the systems to obtain this information for themselves, it is relatively easy for them to share the results that matter with other stakeholders.

Whatever data collection techniques you choose, there are at least four ways to prevent your measurement process from becoming a top-down extractive experience.

1. Know who is going to use the information and how it will be used before you decide to collect it.
2. Think about what is in it for the collectors; how does the information they collect benefit them? How can you help information collectors make the best use of the information they collect to reach their own goals?
3. Make sure the method of measuring helps make progress toward the goal. Does your measurement methodology provide timely feedback that can inform future actions and lead to systems change? Is it creating a new feedback loop in the system?
4. Engage information collectors in interpreting the information that is collected. Do not assume that those who are at a distance from the point of information collection can provide accurate interpretation in the absence of on the ground input.

If you follow these guidelines for your measurement process, it can become a tool for creating meaningful feedback loops that lead to behavioural and systems change.

By supporting transformational measurement processes, YGWYM practitioners *intentionally use the act of measuring to make progress toward their goal*. There is no other measurement process of which we are aware that does this. Rather than treating measurement as proof of an objective truth that exists beyond the influence of human perception, we admit to the fact that measuring something inevitably changes the thing itself. Physicists have a theory about how this works at the quantum level called 'the observer effect', but you do not have to know physics to recognize that the act of measuring can impact what is being measured. For example, to measure tyre pressure, it is necessary to let some air out of the tyre. This affects the precision of the measure. The very act of focusing our attention on the thing that we are measuring elevates it and changes our relationship to it. This is the reason we call this process 'you get what you measure' – our behaviour is influenced by what we choose to pay attention to.

By focusing on transformational measurement, we open up the possibility of focusing our attention in new ways and overcoming the biases we all have to see only what we expect to see. This phenomenon is sometimes called 'selective attention', and is beautifully illustrated by The Monkey Business Illusion video (Simons, 2010). In this video, a group of people are standing in a circle passing a ball back and forth. The viewer is told to count the number of times the ball changes hands. While the ball is being passed around, a person in a gorilla suit walks through the circle. You would think this would be hard to miss but you would be wrong. Most people who watch this video for the first time never see the gorilla. When the video is replayed for them, they are astounded that they missed it. The power of selective attention is extraordinarily strong and is always causing us to miss the things that do not fit our expectations.

Transformational measurement grows out of the process of identifying key leverage indicators in a systems context and allows us to focus our attention on the things we need to see to make better decisions. The fact that measuring itself can change behaviours in the desired direction creates the opportunity to use the act of measuring to move our key leverage indicators in the desired direction.

Direct versus indirect measures

Some things can be measured directly, others only by proxy. The measure of water use cited above is an example of a direct measure. In this instance, it is possible to measure the actual amount of water passing into a given residence and it can be done relatively unobtrusively.

What if your goal was, '**We have a healthy local economy**,' and one of your key leverage indicators was '**More local spending by people who visit our community**'? You might decide to measure the number of people who come from out of town to eat at local restaurants. There are any number of ways you could do this. You could interview customers coming out of restaurants on a regular schedule. You could ask local restaurateurs to collect zip codes from their customers. Both would be direct measures. Another option would be to unobtrusively count the number of out-of-state licence plates in restaurant parking lots on a regular basis. This wouldn't give you as accurate a count, since many people who have in-state licence plates could still be coming in from outside your community, and people in your community may be driving cars with out-of-state licence plates, but it would give you some idea, especially if you did it consistently over a period of time.

Indirect measures are typically not as precise as direct measures, but the trade-off between precision and ease of measuring may be worthwhile. After all, do you really need to know exactly how many out-of-towners there are, or are you more interested in their patterns of use and general trends? The idea is **to match your measure to the level of precision you and others need to make better decisions**. It is better to have approximate knowledge of something that is relevant to your key leverage indicator than to have accurate knowledge of something that is irrelevant. Too often we rely on existing and readily available information that is not the information we really need to make better decisions. YGWYM asks us to push beyond the limitations of existing data if we need to.

Direct or indirect measures could help you establish a baseline. After that, you might devise a clever way to re-measure that would also move your indicator in the right direction. For example, you might organize the restaurants in your community to accept coupons from people who come from outside the community and help them to distribute those coupons widely. To redeem the coupons, customers might be required to fill in their zip codes. The restaurants would learn important information about where their customers come from so that they could better target those markets, in turn creating a direct benefit to them for collecting the information. Once they have systems in place to collect the information on a regular basis, it is a fairly simple matter to ask that they provide this valuable information to the group concerned about the town's economy, particularly if the group is helping distribute the coupons and is planning to share its aggregate findings with participating restaurants. This type of reciprocal relationship around data collecting builds trust and helps move the indicator toward the goal.

Using coupons to attract customers and as a vehicle to collect data relevant to the status of a key leverage indicator is an example of a measurement process that helps move the indicator in the direction of the goal. Installing water meters to measure water use where water use decision-makers can see them is another example. Simply having conversations with intermediaries or information gatekeepers about the YGWYM process, the goals, and the key leverage indicators can also lead to systems changes and changes in the flows of information that can create virtuous cycles. Designing measurement processes that move key leverage indicators in the direction of the goal is a creative process that supports innovative thinking. YGWYM lays the groundwork for innovative measurement processes by including diverse stakeholders from the very beginning of the process. As you gain more experience with YGWYM, your experience as a Measurement Guide can be a tremendous asset in drawing out innovative thinking from diverse stakeholders.

Now that you know what goes into a measurement plan and the aim of the measurement process, it is time to consider which methods of measurement will best suit your situation.

Notes

1. Vermont Environmental Consortium, <https://www.vectogether.org/> [accessed 14 February 2020].
2. A wealth creation value chain is a set of relationships among the people and businesses whose skills and contributions are essential to produce a good or service valued by buyers in the market. A wealth creation value chain achieves financial profitability while building stocks of eight forms of wealth essential for a sustainable and resilient economy. For more information, please see *Wealth Creation: A New Framework for Rural Economic and Community Development*, by Shanna E. Ratner.

References

Ratner, S.E. (2020) *Wealth Creation: A New Framework for Rural Community and Economic Development*, Routledge Publishing, New York.

Rubiner, B. (2007) *Strengthening Rural Families By the Numbers: Using Data to Drive Action on Behalf of Children and Families*, Annie E. Casey Foundation, St Paul, MN. <https://www.aecf.org/resources/strengthening-rural-families> [accessed 29 August 2020].

Simons, D.S. (2010) 'The monkey business illusion' [video]. <https://www.youtube.com/watch?v=IGQmdoK_ZfY> [accessed 8 September 2022].

Tanverakul, S.A. and Lee, J. (2015) 'Impacts of metering on residential water use in California', *Journal of the American Water Works Association (AWWA)* 107(2): E69–E75 <https://doi.org/10.5942/jawwa.2015.107.0005>.

CHAPTER 9
Getting the information you need

This chapter covers alternative methods for collecting information, 'rules' for collecting information, advice for working with secondary data and intermediaries (those who control information you would like to access), and the value of testing measurement plans.

Measurement methods

There are a variety of ways to go about measuring or monitoring behaviour. The four basic methods are: 1) unobtrusive methods that depend on observation rather than interaction; 2) participant observation in which researchers participate in a given activity or setting as observers who take note of what is going on inside and around them as they participate; 3) participatory research (also called participatory action research) in which members of the group or groups whose behaviour you wish to influence participate in doing their own research; and 4) asking questions.

Whether you select unobtrusive measures, participant observation, participatory research, asking questions, or some combination of the above, your choice of research method should always begin with the definition of terms in your key leverage indicator. That will tell you specifically what you need to count or assess or monitor. Once you know what to count, you can then consider how best to count it. Let the key leverage indicator be your guide, not the method. Just because you may prefer one method over another or are more experienced in one method than another does not mean that is the most appropriate way to proceed.

Unobtrusive measures

The term 'unobtrusive measures' was first coined by Webb, Campbell, Schwartz, and Sechrest in a 1966 book titled *Unobtrusive Measures: Nonreactive Research in the Social Sciences*. Any method that does not involve direct elicitation of data from research subjects can be considered 'unobtrusive'. Unobtrusive measures can be very simple, such as driving along back roads and counting the number of total houses and houses with vegetable gardens to get a sense of the proportion of households that are growing some portion of their own food. However, in today's world with the potential for hidden technologies, drones, and other sophisticated methods of observation, unobtrusive measures can be used in inappropriate and invasive ways. Care must be taken to ensure that the data gathered unobtrusively does not violate the privacy or safety of individuals. Having said that, there are many helpful ways to employ technologies such as sensors to determine how often (and how many) people use a particular hiking trail or roadway or stop at a particular exhibit in a museum, for instance. If sensors are properly maintained and the information that is captured is not personalized, much can be learned about behaviour and behavioural change by reviewing this unobtrusive observational data.

Participant observation

Participant observation is essentially an immersion experience in which the researcher is both participant and observer. Being a participant and an observer at the same time requires some training in appropriate protocols for confidentiality and other matters, but this should not be considered a deterrent and the method is widely used. It is different from unobtrusive observation because the observer is an identified participant in the activity. The benefit of participant observation is that it lets the participant/observer share an experience with other participants that can lead to deeper relationships and better understanding of the circumstances affecting participants' behaviours. If YGWYM participants choose participant observation as a research method, it is important to let other participants know what they are doing and why from the start, and to be sure to preserve confidentiality unless specifically authorized by fellow participants to do otherwise.

Participatory research

Participatory research is an approach that empowers non-professionals to use their own local knowledge to control the research agenda with an eye toward using results to promote changes. Participatory research differs from conventional ways of collecting data in several important ways:

1. In participatory research, stakeholders identify the research questions. In conventional research, an expert researcher identifies the questions.
2. In participatory research, stakeholders carry out research activities, and learn the skills and techniques required to do so. In conventional research, expert researchers do the researching.
3. In participatory research, a wide variety of research methods may be used flexibly and in combination, whereas conventional research is typically restricted to a single approach rigidly applied.
4. In participatory research, stakeholders learn to analyse information they have collected and decide how to use this information in action. Stakeholders own the results of the research process. In conventional research, researchers own the results of the research process and are typically more interested in knowledge for its own sake than in using what they have learned to help stakeholders reach their goals.

In practice, most data collection occurs along a continuum between participatory and conventional methods of collecting data as illustrated by Figure 9.1.

More participatory

Less participatory

Community participants/stakeholders

Object of study	Contributors	Initiators/owners
Initiators/owners	Consultants	Facilitators

Expert researchers

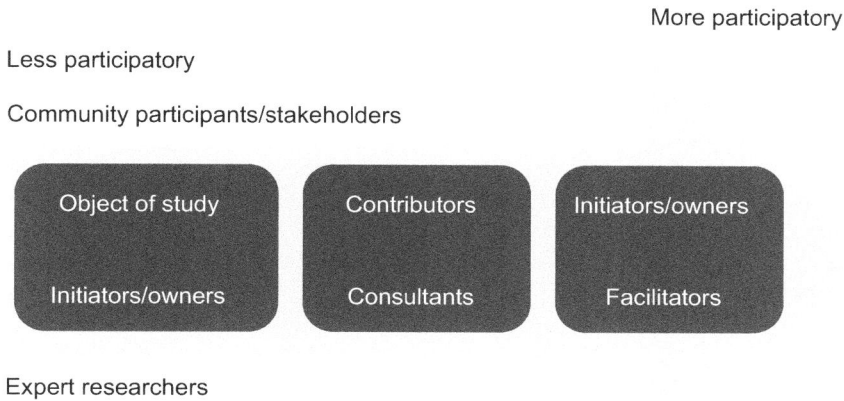

Figure 9.1 Roles in the research continuum

As research becomes increasingly participatory, the role of the expert profes-sional researcher changes. In the most conventional approach, the expert professional researcher initiates and owns the process. In a more participatory approach, the researcher may act as a consultant to those seeking to acquire information. Finally, the researcher may become a facilitator or accompanier to assist others in designing, carrying out, and analysing the results of the research. Community participants change roles as well from being the objects of study to advising and contributing, and finally, to ownership and control of the research process and results. The underlying thrust of participatory research is to involve ordinary people in the process of discovery that is research and to help them use the results of the process to make positive change in their own lives. Participatory research shifts the locus of power from professional researchers to stakeholders.

Participatory research has been in use since the 1940s to help groups of people better understand their own realities and the forces acting upon them. Participatory research emphasizes the importance of reflecting on what is learned so that meaning can be made by those who have conducted the research on their own behalf (Yellow Wood Associates, 2001). Participatory research is dramatically different from the conventional method of extractive research where professionals and/or academics descend on a community or a group of stakeholders to gather information that the professionals will interpret on their own to benefit themselves and their careers.

Participatory research can use many different types of tools, including, but not limited to, photography and videography, mapping, interviews, unob-trusive measures, media analysis, and participant observation or immersion. Many new tools have evolved to make use of computer mapping capabilities. For example, The Green Map Makers, which began in 1992 with a Green Apple map of New York City, has grown into a provider of open source software and instructions for people in over 40 countries who wish to lead local mapping projects that can help them re-envision the places where they live.[1] Local maps have been created linked to transportation, natural infrastructure, toxic chemicals, social gathering places, local food availability, site selection, energy options, and more. The process of mapping reveals important new information to those who undertake it while the resulting maps can provide a powerful way to increase awareness on the part of multiple stakeholders, including decision-makers and others who may not have been engaged in the mapping process of the problem or opportunity.

Similarly, videography is increasingly used to enable stakeholders to investigate and share their experiences from their own perspectives. For example, the Participatory Research Group (PRG) began in 2012 with funding from the UK Government with the intention of bringing the perspectives of poor and marginalized groups to the attention of decision-makers crafting the Sustainable Development Goals (SDGs). Since the SDGs were launched in 2015, PRG has continued to work with marginalized groups in many countries to:

- Bring the perspectives of those living in poverty into decision-making processes
- Embed participatory research in global policymaking
- Use research with the poorest as the basis for advocacy with decision-makers
- Ensure that marginalized people have a central role in holding decision-makers to account throughout the life of the SDGs
- Generate knowledge, understanding, and relationships for the global public good (Institute of Development Studies, n.d.)

Participatory video is one of the methods used by PRG with people living in poverty. As described by PRG:

> Participatory video is an interactive group process, generally facilitated by a practitioner, which aims to build participants' social influence. Group members record themselves and the world around them, and communicate their own stories creatively, but it involves more than collaborative video-making. Practitioners use videoing and playback activities to mediate group discussion inclusively, establish collaborative relationships and catalyse group action. Video production provides a powerful way for participants to explore their situation, and reflect on experiences together, to deepen understanding about reality and forge ways forward based on the knowledge that emerges.

PRG partners with Real Time, an organization based in the UK with extensive experience applying participatory media approaches to research.[2]

The YGWYM process can be conducive to participatory research because it engages a wide range of stakeholders from the start, especially if the advice to include stakeholders who will be impacted by progress toward the goal is followed. (See Chapter Two for more on the types of stakeholders to engage in YGWYM.) Practitioners who use YGWYM are encouraged to consider combining participatory research with other methods. Participatory research can be used in conjunction with expert research and supported by secondary data obtained through negotiations with intermediaries and other information gatekeepers in implementing measurement plans.

Asking questions

Sometimes the best way to figure out what is really going on is to directly ask questions of the people involved. Obvious though this may seem, it is often skipped, especially if those involved are perceived as 'other' or threatening in any way. Asking can be done in person (or via telephone or digitally) or it can be done remotely. When you are asking in person, you have the advantage of seeing and/or hearing the person or people you are speaking with in real time. This means you can test your understanding of what you are being told as well as ask clarifying questions and follow-up questions to go deeper into areas of particular interest. This can be especially useful in testing assumptions that were identified in the indicator analysis.

One of the most popular methods for asking questions remotely is the survey. Surveys can be administered in person, but most often they arrive by mail or electronically and the inquirer never meets the respondent. Surveys are problematic for several reasons. First, no one understands the questions posed in a survey the same way, any more than they understand goals to mean the same thing. If the researcher does not understand how the respondent interpreted the question, there is little way to make sense of the response. This will be true no matter how carefully the wording of the survey is crafted. For example, a question like, 'How effective are the leaders in your community?' begs the question of who each respondent thinks of as 'leaders' and how each respondent thinks of their 'community'. You may think of religious leaders, I may think of volunteer group leaders, and someone else may think of elected officials. You may think of your church group as your community, I may think of my professional relationships, and someone else may think of their town. Given the likelihood of diverse interpretations, it is virtually impossible to make sense of the responses received. The question could, of course, be crafted more precisely, but no matter how precisely crafted, there will always be room for differences in interpretation.

Survey questions can also be misleading, either intentionally or unintentionally. For example, a question about health status might assume that everyone is healthy initially and ignore the impact of pre-existing conditions. Additionally, every survey has margins of error and issues related to the extent to which responders do or do not represent the entire population about which you intend to draw conclusions (also known as response bias). Finally, surveys are ill equipped to appropriately measure human behaviour. People tend to answer the way they think they should, which does not necessarily reflect how they really behave. Since behavioural change is at the core of what we aim to measure we generally encourage Measurement Guides to use surveys sparingly, if at all.

If asking questions is an appropriate measurement method, we suggest you rely on interviews, focus groups, or informal conversations in which the questioner can probe to understand the meaning of the responses to the responder in the context of the responder's reality. Although the number of responses may not be as large, the amount of learning gained from in-person conversations is often much greater.

Rules for getting information

You Get What You Measure offers a chance for ordinary people (stakeholder participants) who are not necessarily trained researchers to engage in data collection (research) which is what you are doing when you implement a measurement plan. There are a few basic 'rules' about getting information that are worth knowing at the outset.

1. *Know that information exists on almost everything.* This was true even before the advent of the internet and big data and is only more true today. Unfortunately, a lot of information is proprietary or protected, even if it is 'public information' in theory. If you are seeking government information in the US, you may want to investigate the Freedom of Information Act, a law that requires full or partial disclosure of previously unreleased information and documents controlled by the federal government on request. All states also have freedom of information laws at state and local levels, though the provisions of these laws vary considerably by state. Every country has their own laws impacting the ownership and availability of information.

2. *Do not give up if you discover that the information you are after is considered 'proprietary'.* If you are fortunate, you may be able to forge alliances with controllers of proprietary information, especially if they share your goals and you can explain why you want the information and how it will be used. The YGWYM process can be shared with information gatekeepers to give them insight into your thinking and what you are trying to achieve.

3. *Remember that information is often contradictory.* What you find out from one source may be different from what you find out from another source. Sometimes these differences are illusory and vanish when time frames, geographies, or other differences in data collection methods or other variables are considered, but sometimes they are harder to explain. Data gains credibility by using the technique of triangulation in which you seek information on the same topic from multiple sources rather than relying on a single source or arbitrarily choosing between two seemingly contradictory sources.

4. *Do not be afraid to collect your own information.* You do not need to have a PhD to measure the things that are most relevant to your key leverage indicators. Collecting your own information will teach you a great deal about the nature of the realities you would like to impact and will allow you to directly test many of your assumptions. This, in turn, will allow you to craft more effective actions going forward.

5. *Remember that the information you think will be 'easy' to obtain often proves to be most difficult and the information you think will be 'hard to get' proves to be relatively simple.* Do not fall into the trap of deciding not to ask for the information you really need to have to make better decisions because you think it will be hard to get. Remember that changing the flow of information is one of the most powerful ways to change systems. *Always ask for what you really need to know.*

Secondary data and intermediaries

Secondary data refers to data that is collected by a third party and not by the group using the data. Many of the social change efforts supported in our society require recipients of financial support like non-profit organizations, schools, communities, and others to use secondary data (often, but not exclusively, census data) to verify 'neediness' (among other things). Government programmes and many non-profits and foundations use secondary data to target their resources as well as to determine individual eligibility for assistance.

Census data collected by the federal government is an example of secondary data. Census data often hides as much as it reveals. While census data has value at a large level of analysis *if care is taken to understand its limitations*, it is rarely well-suited to understanding conditions in more localized geographies. For example, if you live in a 'poor' census tract, you are unlikely to recognize those residents living in the same tract who are not poor. It often comes as a surprise to find that there are wealthy people living in even the poorest rural communities in the United States.

Those of us in the business of social change need to use the measurement process to uncover new and unprecedented information about the places and conditions we wish to affect. That rarely happens when we rely exclusively on secondary data, particularly when it is collected and/or interpreted by organizations far removed from local realities. If we are not careful, secondary data will simply reinforce our assumptions and blind us to the resources available to promote systems change.

Other types of secondary data include, but are not limited to, data from other government agencies besides the Census Bureau such as the Bureau of Labor Statistics or the Economic Research Service, data from universities and academic journals, industry data from trade associations and other industry groups, and data produced by for-profit and non-profit think tanks.

Relevant secondary data can be quite useful, particularly when it provides information that you lack the resources to acquire on your own. However, if you are going to use secondary data, it is critical that you take the time to understand when and how it was collected, the purpose for which it was collected, and any definitions critical to understanding what it means. For example, if you are using historical data from the United States Department of Agriculture Census of Agriculture, you will want to understand how the definition of 'farm' has changed over time. Without this information, it is quite easy to misinterpret and misuse data that has been collected by third parties.

Luckily, there is often a middle ground between doing one's own data collection from scratch and being able to access data that has already been collected. The middle ground emerges in working with intermediaries. In this context, an intermediary is an organization that serves or otherwise interacts with the population whose behaviour must change to indicate progress. Working with intermediaries to collect relevant information is often much more efficient than doing one's own data collection. Furthermore, intermediaries are generally part of the system that must change to make progress, so the very act of engaging them in relevant data collection can help move the system toward the goal. The YGWYM process will help you recognize which intermediaries are, in fact, stakeholders in the systems change you seek. This may not be obvious until you consider who has or has access to the information you need.

For example, if your goal was, 'Children in our community are well-nourished,' and your key leverage indicator was, 'More children in our community eat at least five portions of fresh fruits or vegetables in school each week,' you could recruit volunteers to try to monitor behaviour in the cafeteria or you could work with kitchen staff and school personnel to develop a system that would help them keep track of servings per child. Such a system could be beneficial to the caterer by revealing which fruits and vegetables are most popular and which regularly go to waste. It could also be helpful to school personnel in identifying the children most at risk of poor nutrition. Partnering with an intermediary like a caterer can reduce the cost associated with information collection and improve service delivery at the same time, thus moving the key leverage indicator in the desired direction.

The first step in working with intermediaries to develop cost-effective information collection systems is to share with them the goal and the key leverage indicator and engage them in designing effective systems. They know what information they already collect. They may have valuable suggestions for how existing information might be tweaked to answer the questions you are posing. For example, if they already pay a vendor to handle composted materials, an analysis of those materials might determine how much is edible waste and figures from the compost vendor might be customizable to reveal the amount of waste per day or per week for an individual school. Learning more about the waste stream may also help develop strategies to reduce food waste while improving nutrition.

As this example shows, there may be more than one relevant intermediary organization (e.g. the caterer and the compost vendor). There are also likely to be different levels at which information is collected. For example, the contract with the composting vendor may be at the level of the supervisory union or the school district, not the individual school. Negotiation may be required to obtain data relevant to the geography or demographic that is the target of your work.

It is not unusual to find that information is already being collected on something relevant to your work, but it is either: 1) not being made available outside the organization that collects it and/or 2) is aggregated in such a way that the distinctions you need to make better decisions are absent. For example, data may be collected from individual schools but only made available at the district level. Or data is not identified by month, but only by quarter, which disguises seasonal variations. Open conversations with data collectors can improve the feedback loops in the systems for all concerned. Sometimes, data collectors are already aware of and unhappy with the limitations of their own systems and can benefit from your advocacy in helping them secure the attention and resources of those who can help improve them. This is another area in which social change agents can find shared interests with intermediaries.

Here are a few questions you might use to sort out which intermediaries to approach as you develop your measurement plan:

1. Whose behaviour needs to change to move the indicator in the desired direction and what would that look like?
2. Who already collects information related to that group and/or that behaviour? If you do not know, this is the time to start asking questions. Who do you think might have an interest in the information you are seeking? Start where you can and follow the leads you are given.
3. What is the highest level of aggregation that will be useful to you in making decisions in relation to moving your key leverage indicator in the desired direction? For example, do you need to understand what is happening with individual students, or would it be more useful to understand the consumption patterns of an entire school district?
4. What are the intermediary organizations trying to achieve? What is their self-interest in having better information to improve their own situation? How can you work with them to improve information flow for mutual benefit? Should they be included as stakeholders in your process?

The process of designing and implementing a measurement plan may seem complicated, but it does not necessarily have to be that way. Remember that the fundamental purpose of measuring is to learn. Learning is a joyful and rewarding activity and the excitement of shared learning can be the glue that holds diverse groups together over time. If you think of measuring as a creative rather than reductive endeavour, you will realize what fun it can be! Choose the measures that will teach you the most about what you do not already know and will help you test your assumptions about what you *think* you do know. Remember to calibrate the level of specificity you require to the challenge at hand. Do not expend resources to obtain a level of detail that is either unrealistic or unnecessary.

Testing the measurement plan

Once you have developed a measurement plan you need to test it out to be sure it will work. Measurement plans can go awry in several ways. First, the information you assume to be readily available may prove to be otherwise. My firm, Yellow Wood Associates, was working with the Plattsburgh North Country Chamber of Commerce many years ago on a project to measure the economic impact of Canadian spending on the North Country economy. At one point we approached the New York State Department of Commerce to see if we could obtain sales tax data by type of establishment for several northern New York counties. Since we knew that each establishment was required to report sales data and remit taxes to the state, we had assumed the data would be readily available. First, we were told we could not have it because of confidentiality concerns. When we pointed out that we were only looking for aggregate data, we were told we could not have it because it could not be broken out by type of establishment. That seemed implausible, so we kept on pushing. After numerous exchanges with staff at the Department of Commerce, we were finally told the real reason why the data could not be provided to us. It turned out that the computers in use by the Department of Commerce in the mid-1990s were from the era of the 1960s. They used punch cards. The amount of time it would have taken to fulfil our request made it untenable. Once we informed our client of the situation, they began a campaign to upgrade the state's systems.

Measurement plans may prove unworkable as first conceived for other reasons as well. For example, the intermediaries you thought would be willing to cooperate might choose not to do so. Sometimes persistence pays off. For example, when a community in Maine was seeking data from the State of Maine regarding the specific pollutants that were causing their beaches to be closed, they were initially told they could not have access to that data. However, they continued to investigate, and they were eventually able to identify the staff person who managed the database that contained the information they sought. When they spoke with this person and explained who they were, why they wanted the information, and how they intended to use it (to figure out how to remove the pollutants in question, improve water quality, and get and keep their beaches open), the staff person agreed to give them the information they sought. The YGWYM process provides you with a clear sense of why you want the information and how you plan to use it that can be persuasive when approaching information gatekeepers or intermediaries.

Another issue may have to do with confidentiality constraints that are difficult to work around. Some sectors, like the health care sector, have particularly stringent confidentiality rules that may make it difficult to obtain the information you seek. The weather may also be an obstacle. This can happen if you are relying on observation of something that might only be present at a certain time of year or is only visible or accessible under certain conditions. For example, suppose you want to measure (observe) the prevalence of vegetable gardens in a community. This will be much easier if you are able to collect data just prior to harvest season than if you try to do it during the winter season. Technology may also be a constraint. The technology you were counting on (e.g. sensors or computer technology) may be unavailable, too expensive, incompatible with existing technology or otherwise not feasible in the situation in which you were expecting to use it. You may not have enough people to do the work. You may not be able to recruit and train enough volunteers for what you have in mind. For all these reasons and more, it makes sense to test your measurement plan at a small scale before scaling it up to where you need it to be. The results of the pilot test will tell you where you need to adjust.

Once you have piloted your plan and made any necessary adjustments, you are ready to complete your baseline and framing measures at whatever scale makes sense for your situation. With a measurement plan in hand and baseline and framing measures completed, you are ready to design actions to move your key leverage indicators in the direction of the goal.

Notes

1. Green Map, <https://www.greenmap.org/> [accessed 15 November 2020].
2. Real Time, <https://www.real-time.org.uk/about> [accessed 20 November 2020]. See also Shaw and Robertson (1997).

References

Institute of Development Studies (no date) 'Participate: knowledge from the margins for post-2015'. <https://www.ids.ac.uk/projects/participate-knowledge-from-the-margins-for-post-2015/> [accessed 12 November 2020].

Shaw, J. and Robertson, C. (1997) *Participatory Video: A Practical Approach to Using Video Creatively in Group Development Work*, Routledge, London.

Webb, E.J., Campbell, D.T., Schwartz, R.D. and Sechrest, L. (1966) *Unobtrusive Measures: Nonreactive Research in the Social Sciences*, Rand McNally, Chicago.

Yellow Wood Associates, Inc. (2001) *What is Participatory Research and Why Does it Matter?* <https://yellowwood.org/assets/resource_library/resource_docs/participatoryresearch.pdf> [accessed 24 November 2020].

CHAPTER 10
Actions – re-measurement – interpretation

When you get to this stage in the YGWYM process, you have determined your goal(s) and the key leverage indicators that will move the entire system toward your goals. You have defined your indicator(s) in measurable terms, and you know your unit of measure and your baseline. You have developed at least one framing measure to illuminate the issue at scale. The question you are trying to answer now is, 'What can we do that will move the measure(s) of our key leverage indicator in the desired direction over a reasonable period of time?'

Taking the time required to go through the entire YGWYM process will create shared language, shared experience, and trust among diverse stakeholders. That makes it easier to agree on, craft, and share responsibility for the implementation of effective actions that move measures of key leverage indicators toward goals and result in systemic changes. This chapter explores how actions are designed to move measures in the desired directions, how to think about re-measurement, and what to consider in interpreting the results of measurement.

Acting for impact

An action or an intervention is something you **do**, in addition to the process of measuring, to make progress toward your goal.

Recall the diagram of the YGWYM process presented in Figure 3.1. In that diagram, intervention or action comes *after* measurement, not before. There is an important reason for this. Creating and implementing our measurement plans including creating baseline and framing measures always teaches us a great deal about the situation or system we are trying to affect. We will never know everything there is to know, but the more we know and the more thoroughly we have tested our assumptions and rooted out those that are misguided, the better our chances of designing interventions that will work the way we wish them to work, while avoiding negative unintended consequences.

Because we live in an action-oriented culture, our tendency is to act and react, rather than explore first, learn, and then act. We tend to assume that we know and understand much more than we really do and then we are surprised and dismayed when our efforts do not produce meaningful results. The YGWYM process is a way to interrupt this cycle and insert focused exploration, learning, and reflection *before, not after, we act*.

Participants often find themselves aligning with each other in new ways once they have worked together to identify the larger system and the key leverage indicators most likely to move the system in the desired direction under current conditions. Most significantly, participants often let go of their predetermined agendas and pet theories as they learn more from other participants and the process itself. Letting go of preconceptions increases the willingness to collaborate and learn together. Time invested in the YGWYM process ultimately results in more focus and effective actions than would otherwise emerge, reduces the amount of backsliding and counterproductive behaviour among participants, and increases the likelihood of mutual and lasting accountability, all with the outcome of producing tangible results.

Here is one account from a trained Measurement Guide who used YGWYM to create a community of practice and increase the capacity to conduct evaluations across the Extension Service in the United States. 'Once we completed the process, the action steps were amazingly easy to implement. That is because you get real buy-in about why you are doing these things in the first place as you go along. It makes it so simple because this process goes all the way to action steps whereas other processes do not. With YGWYM, you are past the point of fighting when you get to action.'[1] The process of YGWYM creates a sense of cohesion, shared values, and an agreed upon approach to social change among groups of stakeholders who had not experienced this previously.

Designing actions

In YGWYM, we distinguish between two kinds of actions: 1) **informing actions** and 2) **direct actions**. These are in addition to the measurement processes themselves, which, as we have seen, if intelligently designed can be used to move key leverage indicators in the desired direction. If you are in a car that breaks down and you are fortunate enough to have a cell phone (and a connection!) you could call someone to help you, or if you have a flare you could use that to communicate your need for assistance. Or, if you know what the problem is and have the skill and tools to fix it, you could do just that. Calling for help is an example of taking an *informing action* – sharing information by letting someone else know your situation. Fixing the problem yourself is an example of *direct action*. Both sharing information and direct action are likely to be important in making progress toward your goal. Both may have a role in your action plan. The purpose in making this distinction is to help you think broadly and creatively about a wide range of options for action.

By the time you get to designing actions, the diverse stakeholders you engaged in the YGWYM process from the start are likely already beginning to think about what they can do individually and together to move the system in the desired direction. A wise practitioner once told me that there are two kinds of people attracted to social change work, the *hands* and the *mouths*. The *mouths* are the people who like to meet, talk, and strategize, and the *hands*

ACTIONS – RE-MEASUREMENT – INTERPRETATION   **125**

are the people who like to act. Including some direct actions in your action plan will keep the *hands* engaged.

In social change work, the most powerful actions are often those that bring together organizations that have not previously worked together into a collaborative relationship as partners. Shared participation in the YGWYM process lays the groundwork for unusual collaborations. You may also have recognized opportunities to connect with additional partners beyond the stakeholders who have been involved in your YGWYM process up to this point. *Fortunately, the YGWYM process is easy to document and can be readily explained to new people and organizations with whom you may want to engage around actions.* (See Chapter Six for more on capturing the results of the indicator analysis.)

Informing actions

In considering which informing actions may be most useful in moving your key leverage indicators in the desired direction, you first need to consider the type of information that would be most salient to decision-makers (including yourselves) *that you and/or they do not already have.* Sharing new information or sharing available information in new ways or to new people creates new patterns of information flow which is one powerful way to change systems and behaviours. As we have seen, the measurement process itself can do this and the information derived from measuring can be used as content in informing actions.

Sometimes, the type of research that goes into establishing framing measures can be used to initiate powerful informing actions. For example, if your key leverage indicator was '**More affordable energy efficient housing is available in our region**,' you may choose to conduct research that reveals the proportion of affordable energy efficient housing per household in your region as compared to that in other regions. This will help you frame the scale and scope of the opportunity. Sharing this information with utility companies and/or your state department of energy would be an informing action that may lead to a reallocation of resources. You might also undertake 'best practices' research to identify places, even perhaps in other parts of the world, that have a significantly higher proportion of housing that is affordable and energy efficient than yours does. Once you have identified these places, you can find out what they have done to create the conditions for success. You may even be able to form relationships with people and organizations in these successful regions who can help you adapt the lessons they have learned to your own situation and help you avoid false steps. What you learn through this process can be part of an information action that provides new information of value to multiple stakeholders and potential stakeholders in the YGWYM process.

Depending on the nature of your goal and the stakeholders you have engaged, simply bringing stakeholders' stories to the attention of decision-makers can be a compelling action. For example, when the National Network of Forest Practitioners, American Forests, and other community forestry groups were working with Congress to establish forest stewardship legislation, they brought forest-based practitioners from across the country to testify in front of Congress. Practitioners' stories of their experiences on the ground introduced new information and insights to Congress, which ultimately resulted in legislation to enable forest stewardship programmes to be funded and administered through the US Forest Service.

Think about what new information you could share, and with whom, that would provide feedback that does not currently exist and compel a needed change.

Direct actions

Direct actions, like fixing a flat tyre or sewing masks or renovating a building for a new use appeal to people who like to get their hands dirty. What direct action(s) do you need to take to move the measure of the key leverage indicator in the desired direction so that the indicator will help move the entire system toward the goal? How do you need to shape your actions so that the actions you take are consistent with the goal you are trying to achieve?

Box 10.1 Framing a direct action to achieve a goal in the Virgin Islands

A group of stakeholders in St Thomas, Virgin Islands, came up with a goal: **'Our island's people embrace moral living/virtues.'** One of the key leverage indicators was, **'A more healthy and sustainable physical and social environment**.' One direct action the group came up with was regularly scheduled clean-ups for beaches throughout the island organized and carried out by members of local communities according to a shared protocol. The clean-up activity would provide a baseline and ongoing measure of the cleanliness of the beaches (an important contributor to both the physical and the social environment of the island), but, as importantly, it would actively engage residents of all ages in an ongoing act of stewardship that would demonstrate moral living. This ongoing stewardship of the beaches would be intended to convey the message that the people of the islands care about the resources that nurture them and take their role as stewards seriously because it is the right thing to do. They expect others, for example tourists, to do the same.

To maintain a strong connection between the action, the indicator, and the goal, it would be important to present the beach clean-up activity to participants as being about more than simply clean beaches or environmental protection; the purpose of the activity is to demonstrate moral behaviour with respect to the natural resource base. This is a good example of a situation in which how the action is framed, spoken about, and carried out is as important as the activity itself (i.e. cleaning the beach).

When the citizens' group interested in the impact of upstream factory discharges on downstream water quality took the results of their amateur but compelling measurements to state authorities, this was an example of an informing action directed at key decision-makers. When the food hub in Michigan trained staff throughout their organization to be able to make speeches that told their story, that was an example of direct action. They recognized that developing staff storytelling skills was a prerequisite for getting their story out more broadly.

Educating others as an informing action

It is remarkable how often groups of stakeholders will decide that the most important action they can take is to 'educate' people. This could be thought of as an informing action, depending in part, on whom it is directed toward and how it is carried out. The more targeted it is, the more likely it is to make a difference. And yes, there are many circumstances in which people lack the basic information they need to better understand the situation in which they find themselves. But how will you know if your efforts to educate have been effective?

The impacts of 'education' can seem notoriously difficult to measure, but they do not have to be. Often the measures of success are limited to the number of people who are exposed to your message. However, if you measure success based on the number of people you reach and/or the number who attend your trainings or view your video you will not be able to connect your activity to the behaviour change required to make progress toward your goal. Simply counting the number of people who attend or participate is not an effective way to structure and assess social change. Remember, social change is ultimately behavioural change. Behavioural change is easier to measure than changes in perception or attitude. If attitudes have changed, but behaviours have not, your action has not achieved the desired results.

If your planned actions include an element of education or training, there are ways to structure those actions that are most likely to result in behavioural change. The first step is to target those whose behaviour you are seeking to change. This may seem obvious, but often groups fail to define the audience for their education and revert to broad strokes like 'the general public'. This is analogous to trying to define terms in a key leverage indicator by using dictionary definitions. It will not get you far. Until you have an idea about whose behavioural change will have the greatest impact on progress toward your goal, you are not ready to proceed.

The second step is to let the members of your target audience who participate in your 'education' or 'training' efforts know that your goal is to change their behaviour. Do not hide your intentions. Be clear about what you are trying to achieve and why. This will attract people who see the potential value in changed behaviours. These are the early adopters you need to begin to shift the norm. Screen your participants to establish baseline behaviours relevant to your key leverage indicator and your goal. This does not have to be complicated. You can simply ask for self-reports. If resources permit, you may choose to employ other research techniques as well (see Chapter Nine for some ideas). But it is important to know what the baseline behaviours were before you acted, that is, before you provided education or training.

The third step is to let participants know that you will be checking back with them after a suitable period to see if their behaviour has, in fact, changed. This reinforces the expectation that change will occur. The fourth step is to check back with participants the way you said you would and learn about what and who has changed and what and who has not and why. This information can help you revise your approach to make it more effective. Taking these steps greatly increases the likelihood that the education or training action you develop will lead to behavioural change that moves the key leverage indicator in the right direction.

Once you have identified all the informing and direct actions required to move the measures of your key leverage indicators in the desired direction, compile them into a draft YGWYM action plan and add it to the YGWYM measurement plan. The draft action plan should include informing and direct actions organized by measures of key leverage indicators (ideally no more than three) in relation to goals. Each action should be described in relation to the measure it is designed to move.

Making room for YGWYM actions

Most people and organizations who choose to engage in social change work are already trying to do too much. Their plates are often full to overflowing. The step where actions are designed is the place in the YGWYM process where participants are encouraged to reflect on how they are currently spending their time versus how they will need to be spending their time if they are going to move one or more key leverage indicators in the desired direction. It is not realistic to assume or presume that new actions can simply be added to existing commitments. Instead, it is important to evaluate existing commitments and determine which ones contribute to the new set of actions, which ones could be tweaked to contribute, and which ones should be stopped.

We have developed a simple process to assist with this reflection.

This exercise can help maintain the momentum that develops during the YGWYM process and prevent the return to 'business as usual' as soon as participants return to their offices or as soon as Monday morning rolls around. It can also lead to interesting insights into opportunities for collaboration and/or work sharing among participants and their organizations and reduce duplication of effort.

For example, when we engaged in YGWYM with the Vermont Department of Education, one of the insights gained by various stakeholders was the amount of time they were spending in meetings that had no obvious impacts

✎ Exercise 10.1 Aligning YGWYM actions with current activities

Objectives:

- To reflect on current actions in light of actions prioritized through YGWYM
- To strengthen the connection between existing actions and prior commitments and actions prioritized through YGWYM
- To identify existing actions and prior commitments that can be let go, modified, or delegated to free up resources to pursue priority actions identified through YGWYM

Materials: YGWYM measurement plan and action plan

Time: A minimum of one hour. Will vary by stakeholder and according to the scope of the YGWYM action plan.

Procedure:

1. Make sure each stakeholder has the most recent version of the YGWYM measurement and action plan.
2. Have each stakeholder or group of stakeholders make a list of the items on their own 'to do' lists over the next six months to a year. Begin with the ones that are the most time-consuming. Sometimes it is helpful to break this down into how they spend their time on a daily or weekly basis to get a realistic idea of how they currently allocate their resources. Sometimes it also makes sense to do this from the perspective of an organization overall.
3. Once the list is as complete as they can make it, recognizing that there will likely be some uncertainty the further ahead they look, go on to the next step in the assessment. Have each stakeholder ask themselves, 'Is this activity that consumes x amount of my time connected in any way to the actions we are proposing to move the key leverage indicator in the desired direction?' If the activity in question is strongly connected and well-structured to support or contribute to the proposed actions, put a star next to it. If it could be tweaked to become strongly connected by, for example, including additional stakeholders or changing the timing of it or adjusting the content focus, put a triangle next to it. If it is not connected in any way to the proposed actions, put a minus sign next to it. Proceed through every activity on each stakeholders' 'to do' list in this fashion.
4. Next, go back to those time-consuming activities that have no relation to the actions needed to move the key leverage indicators in the desired direction. Have each stakeholder ask themselves (and/or their colleagues, bosses, funders, etc.), 'Can we stop doing this for the next relevant period (or permanently) and reallocate the freed-up resources to the new proposed actions? If not, can we reduce the time that we are putting into it? If the activity is essential and must continue, is there another group besides ours that would be better suited to carrying it out so that we can focus on the actions that have been identified through YGWYM?'
5. Have stakeholders share the results of their assessments and use these to prioritize informing and direct actions based on available time and resources.

on the key leverage indicators. Once they had the chance to reflect, they were able to identify some areas where time and resources could be effectively redirected and others where simply tweaking the activity by changing its focus slightly or changing who participated would connect it much more strongly to the key leverage indicators and the goal. Seeing these possibilities made the likelihood of follow through far greater than it would have been without taking the time to reflect on current and proposed activities.

Once all the stakeholders have completed and shared their reflections, complete the YGWYM action plan by assigning responsibility for specific informing and direct actions. Include the anticipated time frame for completion, and the time frame for reporting back to the group about the process of implementation and lessons learned.

Re-measurements

The measurement process created through YGWYM is not intended to be a one-time event. Rather it is intended to foster a culture of paying attention to the relationship between actions and behavioural change and of thinking upstream to find the leverage points in a system. The expectation is that re-measurement will occur as needed to determine 1) whether and to what extent progress is being made and 2) what is and is not working and why or why not, allowing the opportunity to re-evaluate and modify actions.

How often re-measurement occurs should be determined based on the nature of the key leverage indicator, the actions selected to move it in the desired direction, and a reasonable estimate of the time it will take to implement those actions and generate measurable changes in behaviour. For example, Colin Novick describes a habitat restoration project in Massachusetts that began in 1997 and has continued through various phases. The original goal of the project was to create a desirable habitat for specific key indicator species of birds. Along the way, many members of the community were involved, invasive tree populations were reduced, and other forms of wildlife were returning. But it was not until 2012 that the question was asked whether the original list of key indicator species of birds had returned. The group with the answers was a local group of birders who, unbeknownst to the site management staff, had been keeping records of species spotted at the site. Their documentation proved the success of the endeavour in achieving its stated goal (Novick, 2020). Had the question been asked too soon, before the habitat was fully restored, there might not have been such clear evidence of success.

Of course, the measurement process itself and the creation and sharing of information about baseline measures can sometimes lead to behavioural change in the relatively short term and re-measurement may be justified to capture these changes. However, all too often, re-measurement schedules are established bureaucratically from the top down and do not reflect realistic time frames for meaningful change to occur. Social change is not a 'project'; it is a living, breathing process that unfolds on its own schedule.

When re-measurement occurs before there is anything there to measure, it is like pulling the plant up by the roots to see how it is growing. Results can be unnecessarily disappointing. Worse yet, the focus on the goal may be lost entirely as practitioners revert to measuring inputs (e.g. meetings held, dollars invested) instead of outcomes (behavioural changes). This is often what happens when social change agents are required to measure their impacts over unreasonably short periods of time. Remember, the primary purpose of measurement in YGWYM is not accountability, but learning. Keep this in mind when considering when and how often to re-measure. Ask yourself, 'How long do we think it will reasonably take to be able to see (and therefore measure) the behavioural changes we seek?' Try not to be pressured into premature re-measurement. At the same time, allow for the fact that some things may change more quickly than you think! Also, keep in mind the capacities that have been intentionally created within stakeholder groups to gather the information they need to make better decisions. Align the capacity and interests of stakeholder groups with the re-measurement schedule as much as possible, keeping in mind how the results of re-measurement will be used. If the changes you seek are likely to take a substantial amount of time, be sure you build in the capacity for ongoing communication and periodic check-ins among stakeholders to maintain focus and engage in learning and reflection to improve impacts over time. Ongoing communications and periodic check-ins offer the opportunity to engage new stakeholders and/or new staff hired by existing stakeholders and spread the culture of the YGWYM approach. It is important to keep a written and visual record of the YGWYM process so that new stakeholders can be brought up to speed and better understand how the focus of the group was determined.

Changing measures over time

Sometimes the measure you begin with will prove to be inadequate, inappropriate, or otherwise misleading as your understanding of the situation improves and/or as circumstances change around you. Do not be afraid to change measures if this happens. Life is unpredictable and uncertain and there is nothing to be gained by imposing consistency where it makes no sense. While continuity has value, that value must be balanced with relevance. Longitudinal comparisons of irrelevant or outdated measures are not helpful. The story of how you got to useful measures over time is. When changing measures, the most important contribution you can make is to record the reasons for the change and explain how the new measure will provide better information for decision-making going forward.

The original goal of Fahe's affordable energy-efficient housing value chain was green affordable housing. Only after multiple interactions with stakeholders did they come to realize that no one really cared about whether their housing was 'green', but they did care about whether it was energy efficient. Henceforth they focused on measures of energy efficiency instead of 'greenness'.

It is also possible that a significant shift will occur in the system of indicators that causes the group to want to rethink their focus. Such a shift can come in many forms that could include, but not necessarily be limited to a change or shift in legislation that opens or closes new doors, the overall economic climate like a market crash, regional demographics, a natural disaster, or cultural priorities as with the Me-Too movement and Black Lives Matter. If such changes occur, YGWYM provides the tools to go back to the beginning and re-identify leverage points for change given the new reality.

Interpreting the results of measurement

Once measurement occurs, whether it is the first time (which may be when the baseline is established) or after subsequent re-measurements, the YGWYM stakeholders come together to reflect on what they have learned. This reflection is a critical part of the YGWYM process and sets the stage for improving actions to make even greater progress toward the goal.

Measures do not speak for themselves. They require interpretation. The most valuable part of any report on measurements is not the numbers but the story behind the numbers. The story, including what is being measured, why this measure is relevant to the systems change you seek (i.e. how it is related to the goal and the key leverage indicator), the baseline conditions, the framing measure, how measurement occurred, what else was happening at the time, and the relative reliability of the results based on the data collection processes used, allows others to make sense of the measure itself.

There are many measures we refer to in our everyday lives without understanding what they mean. One such measure is the unemployment rate calculated by the US Bureau of Labor Statistics. Most people assume that the unemployment rate accurately reflects the percentage of the labour force that is not working. Not so. The unemployment rate only counts people as part of the labour force if they are actively seeking employment. In a period of economic dislocation, such as the one caused by COVID-19, there are millions of people who would be ready and able to join the labour force if employment was available to them; but it isn't, and they have stopped looking for it. They are called 'discouraged workers'. When you subtract the millions of discouraged workers from the labour force, the unemployment rate looks much lower than it would otherwise. This creates cognitive dissonance when people hear that, on the one hand, the unemployment rate is low and, on the other hand, there are more people unemployed than ever before in recent history. If we are going to use measures to make better decisions, we need to understand what they are really telling us, not what we think they should be telling us or what we would like them to be telling us.

Who constructs the measurement narrative matters. One of the strengths of the YGWYM process is certainly in bringing diverse stakeholders together to define a common goal but also to review and reflect on the results of initial measurement and re-measurement. Stakeholders, not an outside third party, should be the ones who work together to interpret the meaning of the measures they chose and whose terms they defined. Stakeholders who are part of or knowledgeable about the population whose behaviour is being measured may have important insights into why the measures are what they are. Was there a weather event, a social event, a disaster, a policy change, or other event of significance that influenced the results? Did the action taken under the guidance of the group have a direct impact or were there other activities that either undermined or accelerated the impact of the group's actions? What were they?

All things being equal, the more that these stakeholders are involved in interpreting the results of measurement, the more likely the interpretations are to capture something real. However, all things are never entirely equal. This is where the contributions to interpretation by stakeholders who represent other constituents is also important. Their questions, observations, and push back can help reveal the larger system in which the measurement results should be understood and will guard against interpretations that are purely self-serving and not necessarily valid. The input of a diverse group of stakeholders in interpreting measurement also guards against confirmation bias: the tendency to interpret new evidence as confirmation of one's existing beliefs or theories. Another safeguard against confirmation bias happens when the YGWYM group revisits the assumptions embedded in and identified during their own indicator analysis when considering the information generated through measurement.

A note on adding it all up

Sometimes the things being measured are the same across the board. For example, if as part of your measure you are measuring pounds of meat purchased from local producers, pounds are a standard measure and could be added across many different producers. However, not all measures are or need to be additive. For example, if you are measuring progress across several key leverage indicators, instead of trying to add up apples and kumquats or convert apples to kumquats (good luck with that!), you could use a simple scale to tell you whether there has been change and if so, if the change was minor or major based on criteria you establish. Stop light colours – red for no change; yellow for some positive change; green for significant positive change (and black for changes in an undesired direction) – can give you a quick dashboard overview of where things stand without wasting resources on trying to establish equivalencies where they do not exist.

Ideally, shared reflecting on the results of measurement should lead to new insights into the larger system. These insights, in turn, can reveal the need for targeted and relevant mid-course corrections in everything from goals, to the definitions of key leverage indicators and even the indicators themselves, and/or measurement plans and action plans. Once your first set of measurement plans and action plans have been implemented, you may want to repeat the entire You Get What You Measure process with additional stakeholders. You Get What You Measure is an iterative process designed to support continuous learning as we strive to improve the complicated and imperfect world we have inherited. Taking the time to truly understand and honour diverse perspectives before leaping into action helps us bring the greatest range of available resources to bear to achieve the changes we want to see.

Conclusion

The YGWYM process is designed to help bring diverse stakeholders into alignment about how to make progress toward shared goals. It can help social change workers develop a much clearer picture of the real scale and scope of changes required to create a more equitable society while at the same time breaking down the silos among and between stakeholders that so often prevent us from making lasting and meaningful progress. The YGWYM process provides a structure in which new and productive relationships are created and maintained as tangible progress is measured and the credit for positive change is widely shared.

   If YGWYM were widely adopted by groups seeking social change we could change our culture to one where more people naturally begin to think in systems, relate their actions to their goals, learn to distinguish upstream from downstream effects, and identify leverage points. The new culture would reward curiosity and normalize identification and testing of assumptions. It would also help to eliminate extractive and exploitative approaches to information collection. Investments in actions and interventions that are not clearly connected to achieving shared goals would be reduced and more resources would be directed to high leverage actions strongly connected with shared goals. Systems of measurement that foster reflection at all levels of society would become a new normal, encouraging learning and continuous improvement. We would have a shared vocabulary to speed our collective learning about best practices.

   I believe the result would be much stronger collaborations, more measurable progress and a more rapid ascent up the steep learning curve facing those of us who sincerely strive to make the world a better place. The more people who understand the process well enough to guide others through it, the faster these cultural changes can occur.

   Congratulations! You are well on your way to becoming a Measurement Guide. Measurement Guides are the facilitators of the You Get What You Measure process. The next step in becoming a Measurement Guide is to try the process out with the group(s) of your choice. The group you choose to work with will bring their own content to the process. Regardless of content, the process remains the same. The more experience you gain with the process, the more confident you will become.

Note

1. Interview with K. Norris, PhD MEd, Senior Evaluation Specialist, 26 June 2020.

Reference

Novick, C. (2020) 'Restoring wildlife habitat in an urban forest', *Northern Woodlands*, Winter 2020. <https://northernwoodlands.org/knots_and_bolts/wildlife-habitat-urban-forest> [accessed 7 December 2020].

APPENDIX 1
Causal looping

Causal looping is a technique used to foster systems thinking. The indicator analysis process used in YGWYM is deliberately inclusive of a wide variety of indicators and therefore not as targeted as causal looping, but it uses the same essential logic by asking about the impact that a change in one indicator is likely to have on another. We introduce the causal looping technique to Measurement Guides so that they can strengthen their own skills as systems thinkers. The author was first introduced to causal looping as a systems thinking tool by The Sustainability Institute as part of her Donella Meadows Systems Thinking Fellowship.

Causal loops are diagrams used to examine the relationships between variables in a system. There are five basic elements of a causal loop diagram: the name of the loop, the variables, the links between the variables (arrows), the signs on the links that show how one variable impacts another, and the sign on the entire loop that identifies what type of loop it is.

There are two types of causal loops: reinforcing loops and balancing loops. Reinforcing loops tend toward unrestrained or exponential growth and balancing loops tend to oscillate around a core value. Reinforcing loops may also be called vicious cycles, virtuous cycles, bandwagon effects or snowball effects. Balancing loops may also be called self-regulating or self-limiting effects.

Drawing and analysing causal loops helps us understand why systems produce the outcomes they do and where adjustments might be made to change them. The intent of the indicator analysis in YGWYM is to identify virtuous cycles and interrupt vicious cycles and self-limiting cycles that prevent progress toward a goal. It can be helpful for Measurement Guides to understand how a virtuous cycle works and what can change to make it into a self-limiting or vicious cycle.

The first step in building a causal loop is to name the variables. Variable names should be nouns or noun phrases that can go 'up' or 'down' over time. For example, instead of 'farmers grow more corn', use 'corn grown'. Variable names should also convey a clear sense of direction when appropriate; for example, not 'word of mouth' but 'positive word of mouth'.

The second is to link the variables and describe the nature of the relationship between them. The link between variables describes the impact of one variable on the next. Variables may change in the *same* direction such that when A increases, B increases, all else being equal, and when A decreases, B will tend to decrease, all else being equal. Or variables may change in the *opposite* direction such that when A increases, B decreases and vice versa, all else being equal. When drawing a causal loop, each link or line between two variables is labelled either 's' meaning the two variables move in the same direction, or 'o' meaning the two variables move in opposite directions.

The third step is to label the type of loop. Causal loops can have many or few variables. To characterize the loop one looks only at the 'opposite-type' relationships. Regardless of the number of variables, **reinforcing loops** either have no variables moving in the opposite direction or they have an even number of variables moving in the opposite direction. **Balancing loops** have an odd number of variables moving in the opposite direction.

The final step is to name the loop so that you are clear about the context within which your analysis applies (Lannon, 2018).

Here are a few examples:

Supply demand relationship for corn

The story. Everything else being equal, when the price of corn goes up, the number of acres planted in corn goes up and the amount of corn consumed goes down (o). When the amount of corn consumed goes down, the amount of surplus (or unsold) corn goes up (o). When the amount of surplus corn goes up, the price of corn goes down (o). When the price goes down, the number of acres planted to corn also goes down, consumption goes up and the surplus goes down. As the surplus shrinks, the price goes up, starting the cycle over. This is a balancing loop that fluctuates around a core value.

Virus transmission loop

The story. Everything else being equal (e.g. no vaccines or cures), when the number of people following social distancing protocols goes up, virus transmissions go down (o). When virus transmissions go down, the sense of safety

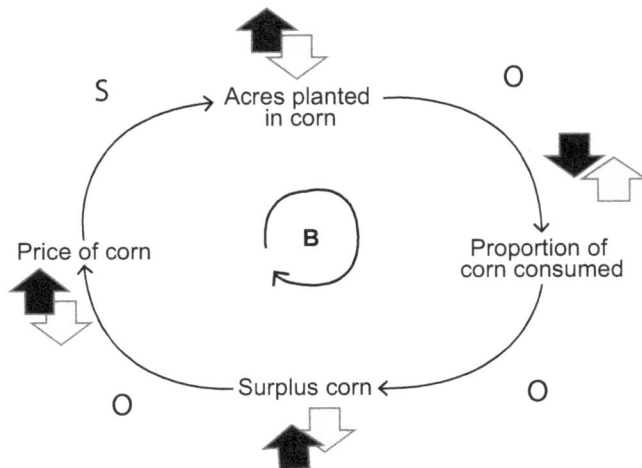

Figure A1 Supply/demand relationship for corn

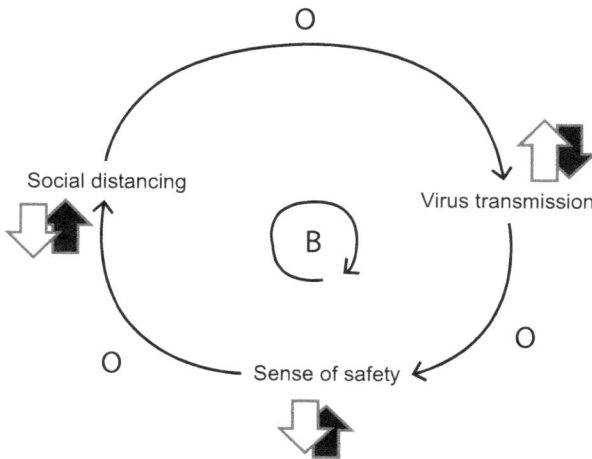

Figure A2 Virus transmission loop

goes up (o). When the sense of safety goes up, social distancing goes down (o). When social distancing goes down, virus transmission goes up (o). When virus transmission goes up, sense of safety goes down (o). When sense of safety goes down, social distancing goes up. This is a balancing loop that fluctuates around a core value.

Exercise loop

The story. Everything else being equal and assuming we are starting from a very small amount of time spent exercising, when time spent exercising goes up, the amount of endorphins released in the body goes up (s). When the amount of endorphins released in the body goes up, the desire to exercise

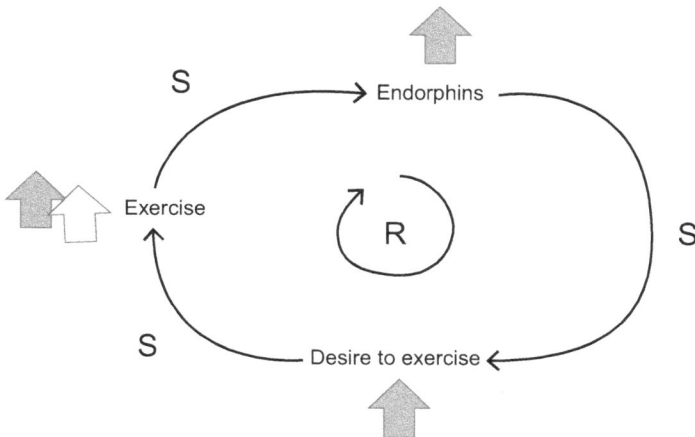

Figure A3 Exercise loop

increases (s). When the desire to exercise goes up, the amount of time spent exercising goes up (s). This is a reinforcing loop that creates a virtuous cycle – the more you exercise, the better you feel, the more time you want to spend exercising. There is, of course, a limit to the amount of time that can be spent exercising, but within that constraint, the virtuous cycle holds.

The best way to understand causal looping is to practise it. Pick an outcome that interests you and tell yourself a story about the relationships between the key variables that you think contribute to that outcome. The outcome could be personal like weight loss, job satisfaction, or a good relationship or it could be social like full employment or water conservation or drug addiction. Name the variables, draw the links and label them, and see if you can figure out what kind of loop you have drawn. Is there another variable you could add (or one you could remove) that would change the dynamic of the loop?

Familiarity with causal looping can be helpful to Measurement Guides as they work with stakeholders to better understand how indicators are connected to goals. It can also be useful in helping stakeholders recognize the virtuous cycles identified through the indicator analysis.

Reference

Lannon, C. (2018) 'Causal loop construction: the basics' [online], The Systems Thinker. <https://thesystemsthinker.com/causal-loop-construction-the-basics/> [accessed 5 December 2020].

APPENDIX 2
Suggestions for implementing the YGWYM approach virtually

This appendix describes how the steps in the YGWYM process can be conducted over the internet using any one of many platforms that are available for group work, such as Zoom or Microsoft Teams. In addition to a meeting platform, the Measurement Guide should choose and familiarize themselves with an interactive whiteboard program. One free version of such a program available at the time of publication is called Jamboard. The basic functionality you will need includes the ability to write and post sticky notes, arrange notes in space, draw and erase coloured lines and arrows with software that all participants can view and, ideally, manipulate as appropriate to each exercise. You will also need to know how to take, save, and share screenshots.

The main differences between conducting YGWYM sessions in person and online are:

1. It will take some time to identify platforms and technologies available to the complete range of stakeholders and prepare instructions on their use as needed.
2. It may be necessary to provide some stakeholders with access to secure and reliable internet and functional computers with cameras and microphones.
3. The success of online work will depend, in part, on stakeholder awareness and skill in online interactions – for example not speaking over each other; muting when not speaking.
4. It may be more difficult for participants to take turns leading exercises online if they are not comfortable with the technology and have not had a chance to practise beforehand.
5. Working in groups online can be more tiring than working in person. The Measurement Guide may need to structure work in smaller time blocks over longer periods of time than would be necessary if working in person. Additionally, some groups may prefer to work in many shorter sessions while others may prefer fewer longer sessions.
6. Online group work sessions can be supplemented by short pre-sessions in which stakeholders receive and clarify instructions for work they can then carry out individually prior to their work together. Online pre-sessions can also be used to introduce key concepts including the

definitions of key terms, and supply participants with written definitions to which they can refer. Pre-sessions and pre-work can shorten the time required for group work online.

Some of the following exercises can be combined with others if time permits. Others can be divided into sections by goal or otherwise if there is a preference for shorter sessions.

Suggestions by exercise

Creating our own ground rules

This exercise can be readily adapted to the virtual environment given the likelihood that most, if not all, stakeholders will have participated in multiple virtual meetings and trainings by the time they become engaged in the YGWYM approach. The only difference would be to emphasize what works well and what does not work well specifically in a virtual environment. You may wish to send the list generated by the group out to all stakeholders and possibly post it in the Chat (or equivalent) at the start of every session.

Skilled inquiry and skilled listening

Both skilled inquiry and skilled listening can be practised in groups of three in breakout rooms using the instructions in Chapter Four.

1. Introduce the exercises to the whole group.
2. Put people into breakout sessions to practise.
3. Use a timer to let them know when it is time to switch roles.
4. Debrief as a whole group.

Everyday measurement

This exercise is easy to translate to the virtual environment, should you choose to include it. Use instructions in Chapter Two.

1. Introduce the exercise to the whole group.
2. Put people into breakout sessions to practise.
3. Use a timer to let them know when it is time to switch roles.
4. Debrief as a whole group.

Generating values to themes

This is the first set of exercises that will benefit from an interactive whiteboard.

1. Begin with an explanation of the process the group will be engaged in and its purpose.
2. Provide written definitions of key term **values** for reference and review.
3. Write instructions into Chat or equivalent and review them.

4. Have each person name a value and write it on the whiteboard. If the application you are using does not make this easy, have each person read their value out loud and have the Measurement Guide write each value on an individual sticky note and post it on the whiteboard for everyone to see. Continue until all the values are posted and everyone has contributed at least one.
5. Allow clarifying questions and a brief discussion of each value as it is posted.

Values to themes

1. Explain the purpose and process for the exercise.
2. Provide written definitions of key terms **values** and **themes** and review.
3. Give instructions and write them into Chat. See Notes below:

   Notes:
   a. *It may not be possible to do this exercise in silence as one would if it were being done in person. If that is not possible, then verbal communication should be kept to a minimum. This is NOT the time to discuss the meaning of values or argue about where they belong.*
   b. *There are several different ways you might group values into themes. One would be to make a screenshot of all the values on the whiteboard and divide the large group into several smaller (10–15 person) working groups, each with their own whiteboard to use for sorting the values into themes. If you do it this way, you will need to allow additional time after the small groups have completed their work to compare the results of each group and adjust as needed; that is, copy values that need to be duplicated and/or divide groups of values into smaller clusters. Another way to proceed would be to work together as one whole group with the Measurement Guide in charge of moving the sticky notes around in response to suggestions from stakeholders. This would probably work if you are working with 20 or fewer stakeholders. For more than 20 stakeholders, you will probably want to divide into smaller groups.*

4. Once the groupings of values are finalized, take a screenshot of each cluster of values.
5. Divide the group into smaller groups of 5–10 people in breakout rooms and have each small group work on at least one and up to three clusters of values and develop a theme for each.
6. Have each group write their theme on a different colour sticky note, or on the whiteboard above the sticky notes, or with a different colour of ink – whatever it takes to differentiate the theme from the values.
7. Come back together as a whole group and complete the exercise by having each small group share the theme and related values for every theme they developed.
8. Allow the whole group to briefly discuss and modify the themes if needed.

Themes to goals

1. Explain the purpose and process for the exercise.
2. Provide written definitions of key terms **values**, **themes**, and **goals** and review.
3. Go over instructions and place them in Chat.
4. Go back into the same breakout groups that developed themes from values and ask them to come up with a goal statement for each theme.
5. Come back together and share goal statements. Revise as needed.
6. Measurement Guide adds a goal statement above each cluster of values with themes on the whiteboard. Save a screenshot for later reference.

Prioritizing goals

1. Discuss the purpose and process that will be used to prioritize no more than three and ideally two goals. These should be the things that have to happen before other goals can be achieved.
2. Present screenshot of goals with values and themes.
3. Assign a letter to each goal.
4. Have the group use a 'raise hands' or a polling process to prioritize goals.
5. Discuss results as a whole group.
6. Consider whether the top two goals are internal or external goals. If both goals are external, consider asking the group, 'What would have to be true of your organization for it to contribute to each of these goals?' Use responses to develop one internal goal. If both goals are internal, ask 'What is the condition in the external world that these internal conditions would help you create?' Use responses to develop one external goal.
7. Write priority goals on the whiteboard and take a screenshot.

Guided visualization

This exercise is easy to translate into the virtual environment. Simply lead the visualization as you would if you were in person and have each participant make notes to themselves for future reference.

Developing and clarifying indicators

1. Describe the purpose and process that will be used to develop indicators.
2. Do this for one goal at a time. Write the goal on the whiteboard.
3. Provide and review a written definition of the term **indicator**.
4. Ask participants to refer to notes from the visualization exercise to develop their indicators.
5. Have participants write their indicators on virtual sticky notes and place them on the whiteboard, or if this is not technologically possible, have the Measurement Guide transcribe each indicator onto a sticky

note as the participant expresses it and post each indicator on the whiteboard so everyone can see all of them.

6. As each indicator is clarified, rewrite the indicator on a fresh sticky note and delete the original version from the whiteboard.
7. Search for exact duplicates. Usually participants will say something like, 'Mine is the same as hers' before stating their indicator. Compare and combine indicators as needed as a whole group and with Measurement Guide help.
8. At the end of this exercise there should only be one of a duplicate indicator on the whiteboard.
9. Take a screenshot of the list of indicators associated with each goal.
10. Repeat for up to three goals. Each goal can be addressed in a separate session if desired.

Everyday assumptions

This exercise translates easily into the virtual environment.
1. Describe the purpose and process for identifying assumptions.
2. Provide a written definition of the term **assumption**.
3. Provide a virtual version of the worksheet.
4. Complete the exercise as a whole group unless there is more than one Measurement Guide, in which case you can break into smaller groups with one Guide per group.

Analysing indicators in a systems context

1. Write the first goal on the whiteboard.
2. Arrange the indicators related to that goal in a circle on the whiteboard.
3. Describe the purpose and process of analysing indicators in a systems context.
4. Post step-by-step instructions in the Chat.
5. Complete the exercise virtually. If technology allows, have participants take turns comparing indicators and drawing arrows. Once you have used all the different colours available for drawing lines between indicators, use different line widths to expand the number of distinct types of lines available.
6. Complete the exercise as a whole group unless there is more than one Measurement Guide, in which case you can break into smaller groups with one Guide per group.
7. Take a screenshot of the result for each goal.
8. Repeat for up to three goals. Each goal can be addressed in a separate session if desired. Additionally, the same goal and its related indicators can be analysed simultaneously by different groups of stakeholders in different breakout rooms if desired. Be sure to take time to bring the whole group back together to compare the results.

Capturing assumptions

If you choose to use breakout rooms for the indicator analysis, be sure there is someone in each room to capture assumptions. Assumptions do not need to be shared as they are being captured. If you use breakout rooms and/or participants share the job of capturing assumptions, the Measurement Guide will want to remind the volunteers to make sure each assumption is clearly connected to the indicator(s) to which it applied. The Measurement Guide should collect all the assumptions and prepare a summary document of all assumptions. Another, shorter, version of this document can be created after key leverage indicators are identified. The shorter document should be used as a reference during the measurement and action-planning exercises.

'Scoring' the indicator analysis

In a virtual setting, the indicator analyses (one or two per goal) can be scored by the groups that completed it using a screenshot of the completed analysis for reference. The entire breakout group can participate in the scoring and scores can be written on the active whiteboard on which the analysis was originally conducted. If each breakout group can have its own whiteboard, so much the better. If not, they can use the screenshot as reference and simply record the scores by indicator and report them back to the Measurement Guide during the next exercise. Using the screenshot as a reference should allow for double checking and limit any premature labelling of the original analysis.

Interpreting the indicator analysis

Once each analysis is scored, each group doing the scoring should share their whiteboard with the whole group or report their scores to the Measurement Guide to post on the central whiteboard.

The remainder of the analysis should be conducted on the central whiteboard so that all participants can see how the leverage indicators for each goal impact the entire system for that goal, as well as the relative strength of each indicator.

The Measurement Guide should record the key results and key leverage indicators for each goal on a central whiteboard.

Once all the indicator analyses have been completed and all the key leverage indicators have been identified, the Measurement Guide can shorten the summary of assumptions to focus on the assumptions related to the key leverage indicators. This can be done offline.

Defining terms in key leverage indicators

1. Write the first goal and its key leverage indicators on the whiteboard.
2. Describe the purpose and process that will be used to define key terms in leverage indicators.

3. Use the whiteboard to indicate which terms are being defined and to capture definitions.
4. Once the whole group has observed and participated in the process for defining the terms in key leverage indicators for one goal, it may be possible to divide the group into breakout rooms to complete definitions for the key leverage indicators related to additional goals. This will work best if each breakout room has its own whiteboard with the goal and key leverage indicators listed on it to start.
5. If some of the work is done in breakout rooms, be sure to share the results back with the entire group.
6. As a whole group, determine and record the unit of measure for each key leverage indicator and take a screenshot.

Beginning at the end by considering how you will use the results of measurement

Once the key leverage indicators for each goal have been identified and the key terms in each have been defined, it is a good time to introduce the different ways in which the results of measurement can be used. Part of this discussion can involve brainstorming ideas for the use of information related to each goal. Ideas can be recorded on the whiteboard and set aside for review and further consideration when it is time to make the measurement plan.

The measurement plan

Measurement plans are best developed offline by mixed groups of stakeholders with guidance from a Measurement Guide. However, introducing the concept of a measurement plan, including units of measure, baselines, and framing measures as well as the variety of ways in which information can be collected, can be done through an online session with the entire group. This is also the time to introduce concepts of extractive versus inclusive measurement, 'rules' for gathering information, and direct versus indirect measures. It may be helpful to share the entirety of Chapter Nine with the stakeholder group ahead of this session. It is also important to bring the summary of key assumptions back into awareness as measurement plans are drafted since the plans provide an opportunity to test assumptions.

After the online introduction and a question-and-answer period, groups of stakeholders can be offered the guiding questions for a measurement plan, a schedule for checking in with the Measurement Guide (which could be done online) and a deadline for preparing a draft plan related to whichever goals and/or key leverage indicators they have been assigned. Once draft measurement plans have been completed, they should be shared with the entire group and an online conversation can be held to accept input and refine the plans prior to testing. This session can also be used to discuss the process and responsibilities for testing the measurement plan for each goal and capturing lessons learned.

Developing the action plan

Action plans are best developed offline by a diverse group of stakeholders with guidance from a Measurement Guide. However, introducing the concept of an action plan, including informing and direct actions and the relationship of actions to measures, key leverage indicators, and goals can be accomplished online. Measurement Guides can provide guiding questions for action plans to assist groups of stakeholders.

After the online introduction and a question-and-answer period, groups of stakeholders can be offered the guiding questions for an action plan with a schedule for checking in with the Measurement Guide (which could be done online) and a deadline for preparing a draft plan related to whichever goals and/or key leverage indicators and measures they have been assigned. Once draft action plans have been completed, they should be shared with the entire group and an online conversation can be held to accept input and refine the plans prior to reflecting and aligning the action plans with current actions.

Aligning YGWYM actions with current actions

The concept and steps for aligning YGWYM actions with current actions can be introduced online.

1. Describe the process and purpose.
2. Provide a written summary of the measurement plan and the action plan.
3. Demonstrate the process and answer questions.
4. Set a timeline for stakeholders to complete their own review of current actions and share findings with the entire group.
5. Finalize the action plan at the next session, incorporating reflections on current actions.

Ongoing communications

Virtual meetings can be an excellent vehicle to maintain ongoing communications among diverse stakeholders. They can be used to provide updates on testing and implementation of measurement plans and action plans as well as lessons learned. They can be used to determine course corrections and revisit assumptions. After baselines are established, actions taken, and re-measurement occurs, they can also be used to bring stakeholders together to discuss the interpretation of results and determine next steps.

APPENDIX 3
Links to video content linked to book chapters

Preface

1. Introduction to Becoming a Measurement Guide (BMG) Workshop Participants
   <https://youtu.be/b7sG6Hvs9Go>
2. Description of the contents and design of the BMG Workshop
   <https://youtu.be/1GiLmfzvCLQ>
3. Questions and Expectations of Workshop Participants
   <https://youtu.be/1e1xuvybfp8>

Chapter One

1. Who to use this process with and the history of YGWYM including the difference between this process and the evaluative approach used by most funders. Also includes a discussion of obstacles to being a learning community and how this process addressed these obstacles
   <https://youtu.be/RRItctJbJtI>
2. When to use this process based on a group's stage of development: forming, storming, norming, and performing
   <https://youtu.be/6XUgcKzzbCo>
3. Generating ground rules for learning to create shared responsibility
   <https://youtu.be/sWSre3dWDho>

Chapter Two

1. Everyday Measurement exercise and debrief
   <https://youtu.be/ncIIKWOwTJw>
2. Stakeholders: a discussion of three categories of stakeholders with examples and discussion of application to internal and external goals
   <https://youtu.be/_Vj2tfi-yZE>
3. Stakeholders continued, and the use of content expertise in the YGWYM process
   <https://youtu.be/gURuPiMUrQs>

Chapter Three

1. Measurement Vocabulary including goal, indicator, assumption, action, and measure
   <https://youtu.be/879iqtFFfYw>

2. Overview of the Measurement Process
<https://youtu.be/Kbo61Zl8ing>
3. Introduction to Skilled Inquiry and Skilled Listening with discussion
<https://youtu.be/qA-ivk_nld4>
4. Skilled Listening and Skilled Inquiry practice session
<https://youtu.be/Fk6y3ZJPZbg>
5. Skilled Listening and Skilled Inquiry practice session and discussion
<https://youtu.be/GsgD5vxq35M>

Chapter Four

1. Introducing the case study and the roles that workshop participants choose for themselves
<https://youtu.be/lr1IQt26_8M>
2. Values to Themes introduction and discussion
<https://youtu.be/xQGR4eA9SOA> and
<https://youtu.be/3rMtr2khelw>
3. Themes to Goals example and discussion, includes discussion of internal and external goals.
<https://youtu.be/sWSre3dWDho>

Chapter Five

1. Visualization introduction
<https://youtu.be/gURuPiMUrQs>
2. Visualization exercise and connection to developing indicators with discussion
<https://youtu.be/iyN7lvStzD8>
3. Indicators, the definition and form of an indicator, developing and clarifying indicators and connecting indicators to goals with examples and discussion
<https://youtu.be/j-Qe6LpsiZ0>
4. Connecting Indicators to Goals: discussion about indicators and making the connections between the indicator and the goal clearer and stronger
<https://youtu.be/LF3CLLtkpyo>

Chapter Six

1. Assumptions: discussion of assumptions and how to set the stage to help people examine them, discussion of doing the Everyday Assumptions exercise as a warm-up for the indicator analysis
<https://youtu.be/vSARkPnUvmI>
2. Indicator Analysis: example of the process of Indicator Analysis based on a fictional case study and role playing by participants
<https://youtu.be/dbl2SdlnDgg>

3. Indicator Analysis continued
   <https://youtu.be/bVCSmYNpTho>
4. Indicator Analysis discussion and interpretation
   <https://youtu.be/g3-sySgmi2o>

Chapter Seven

1. Defining key terms in an indicator: discussion of units of measure and baselines, the importance of choosing stakeholders thoughtfully, timelines for re-measurement, the role of expert opinion and the relationship of measures to actions
   <https://youtu.be/bi_V7baWyPA>
2. Skilled Advocacy: a skill for presenting the results of measurement to influence decision making, examples of participants practising skilled advocacy
   <https://youtu.be/sCcOI027Ep0>
3. Skilled Advocacy continued
   <https://youtu.be/AW7nWYqOuis>

Chapter Eight

1. Measures: discussion of measuring 'goods' versus 'bads,' positive deviance, direct and indirect measures and creativity in measurement, exercise on the difference between indicators and measures, discussion of how many people to include in an indicator analysis
   <https://youtu.be/nOE8UOi4NGk>
2. Dimensions in Measurement: discussion of information you need to make better decisions versus information that would be 'nice' to know and more
   <https://youtu.be/xvm8TfVrVG4>
3. Dimensions in Measurement discussion continued: qualitative versus quantitative data
   <https://youtu.be/ShMLhJjDgL4>
4. Goals, Indicators, and Measures: reviewing the relationship between measures, indicators, and goals, defining the measure and the baseline
   <https://youtu.be/phSpahfxkVE>
5. Framing Measures
   <https://youtu.be/oY52cvE9y_U>
6. Creating a Measurement Plan: identifying the information and information collection systems already in use
   <https://youtu.be/wJSXUAJObFs>

Chapter Nine

1. How to get information: the limitations of surveys and intermediate data sources and institutionalizing data collection
   <https://youtu.be/wJSXUAJObFs>

2. How to get information continued: discussion of the importance of partners, levels of information, levels of aggregation, values of information gatekeepers, how to use the measurement process to make progress toward your goals, what to do if there is no relevant data already available and you will be creating the baseline the first time you measure
   <https://youtu.be/_yT4tSn0fuo>

3. Measurement Methods and rules for getting information
   <https://youtu.be/7lRSH-0qhCs>

Chapter Ten

1. Getting to action, discussion of direct actions and informing actions. Different formats in which YGWYM has been offered
   <https://youtu.be/4KfbySyUnoo>

2. Creating an Action Plan
   <https://youtu.be/wJSXUAJObFs>

3. Using the results of measurement
   <https://youtu.be/ZFihLaqGueY>

4. Aligning actions with Current Activities
   <https://youtu.be/QxpPRw88uSY>

5. Reflections on the in-person training: review of the questions and expectations that participants came in with
   <https://youtu.be/q2tQ5XPh4YU>

6. Interpreting the results of measurement, adjusting measures over time, and a discussion of trusting and learning from the measurement process and self-organization.
   <https://youtu.be/phSpahfxkVE>

Appendix 1: Causal Looping

1. Introduction to Causal Loop Diagrams
   <https://youtu.be/qmGsuJhjlX4>

2. Instruction om Causal Looping continued and Participants' Examples
   <https://youtu.be/VKouSAWUwps> and
   <https://youtu.be/dVNfMUgxVzY>

Bonus videos

1. Stocks and Flows as a key element in systems thinking
   <https://youtu.be/s0YiYhpabCI>

2. The application of You Get What You Measure to wealth creation
   <https://youtu.be/UZEI1cztRfY>

3. Definitions of seven forms of wealth
   <https://youtu.be/E4-QGctYOfw>

4. Cultural capital as the eighth form of wealth
   <https://youtu.be/hYbTonZeVfg>
5. Introducing the Wealth Matrix
   <https://youtu.be/XxobyFoPszA>
6. Use of the Wealth Matrix (continued)
   <https://youtu.be/TIM_ydKVAgE>
7. Commonalities in approaching how to measure different forms of wealth
   <https://youtu.be/FAOZYaACDvw>
8. Structures for local ownership of wealth
   <https://youtu.be/7jHojaHEgwA>

Milton Keynes UK
Ingram Content Group UK Ltd.
UKHW022215180823
426952UK00004B/4

9 781788 532525